Better Homes Cookery

FONDUE and TABLETOP COOKBOOK

Marguerite and Judith Patten

COLLINS LONDON AND GLASGOW

Acknowledgements

	Page	
Spring Brothers	13	Carousel Fondue Set
	17	Beef Fondue Set
	38	Toblerone Set
	45	Flambé Pan
		Candle-type Hotplate
	90	Irish Coffee Warmers
Sunbeam	45	Multicooker
	57	Automatic Frypan : Fish Meunière
	68	Deep Cooker
	89	Electric Percolator
Jobling Housecraft Service	45	Pyrex Casserole
Pifco	45	Twin-Ring Cooking Unit
		Electric Hotplate
Pier-1 Ltd	53	Habachi Grill
Moulinex	53	Rotisserie
Pyrosil	57	Frying Pan on Chrome Stand
	88	Paella
Royal Worcester	60	Flame-proof Casserole
Rima Electric	65	Infra-red Cooker
Russell Hobbs	72	Roaster Toaster
Scottish Milk Marketing Board	75	Welsh Rarebit
	83	Crêpes Suzette
	90	Irish Coffee
Sona	76	Griller Toaster
Husquvarna	85	Waffle Iron
Eden Vale	87	Onion Dip and Tomato Shrimp Dip

Cover photograph by courtesy of
The Milk Marketing Board

Copyright © Meredith Corporation 1970
UK Edition first published 1973
Printed in Great Britain by Collins Clear-
Type Press
ISBN 0 00 435525 3

Contents

Focus on Fondue

Tired of working in the kitchen? Then bring fondue to the table. No need to wait for a party, or for family guests to arrive. Any time is the right time to cook-at-the-table with fondue.

Fondues give menus seemingly new and exciting twists, yet the idea originated long ago. Out of a desire to utilize semi-stale hardened cheese and bread, the Swiss concocted a mouth-watering cheese and wine mixture. The cheese was melted in wine, and the bread cubes were then dunked in the mixture. The name *fondue* came from the French word *fondre* which means 'to melt'.

In this section we have put together the most interesting fondues from appetizers to desserts. You will find suggestions for complete menus that incorporate various kinds of fondue. Experiment with these recipes and you will be delighted with your skill as a fondue hostess.

Some idea of the variety of fondue dishes is shown in this picture, which includes ingredients for meat, cheese, and dessert fondues. A fondue pan, heater and the long-handled forks are essential equipment for all three types.

The ABC of Fondue

Fondue cooking is one of the quickest, easiest, and most interesting methods of preparing food. Check the points on this and the next page for facts, hints, and ideas on using the fondue equipment efficiently and safely.

1 *Above: a metal fondue pan, ideal for cooking meat fondue etc, with the heater, heat-proof tray and sectioned plate for the food.*

2 *Opposite left: A small pot, ideal for dessert fondues.*

3 *Far right: A ceramic pot, ideal for cheese or sauce-type fondues. The wide shape enables you to swirl the bread or dipper in the mixture.*

FONDUE EQUIPMENT

There are many fondue sets now on the market. Each set includes all or most of the following items :

THE CONTAINER in which the food is heated. This is generally called the fondue pot or pan, and it can be of metal (stainless steel, enamelled steel, cast-iron, or copper) or strong ceramic ware (pottery or the ware often described as 'flame' or 'heat' proof).

If you wish to buy just *one* pan in which to make all types of fondue, choose a *metal* pan, for this withstands very high heat and is essential for fondues that must be cooked in hot oil (meat fondues, etc). It can be used also for cheese and dessert fondues.

Ceramic pots cannot be used for heating oil to a high temperature as they may crack, but they are perfect for cheese and dessert fondues.

Choice of shape: The shape and gauge of metal containers are important. A bowl-shaped pan that is larger at the bottom than at the top minimizes oil splattering (see opposite page and sketch 1). A heavy gauge ensures even heat distribution.

Ceramic pots most closely duplicate the original Swiss *caquelon* used for cheese fondue. Shaped like a shallow casserole dish with a handle, the pot's added surface area provides the room needed for swirling a cheese or sauce-type fondue. Similar pans, often in a smaller size, are ideal for desserts.

Number of pans: Allow one fondue pan for every four to six persons when serving a hot-oil fondue, for the oil will not stay sufficiently hot to cook food for more than this number at one time. When making cheese, sauce or dessert fondues one pan can serve six to eight people.

THE STAND upon which to balance the pan over the heater. Always check that the pan is evenly balanced on the stand.

THE HEATER This can be a methylated spirit heater or a candle (night-light) heater. The former is essential for keeping the hot oil at the right temperature or for melting the cheese mixture. A candle-type heater is only adequate for keeping sauce fondues warm.

The heater must be put on to a metal stand to ensure that the heat does not harm the table. Often a stand is supplied with the fondue set.

FONDUE FORKS may be included with the complete set or you may have to buy them separately. These forks hold the meat, fish, bread, or other food to dip into the hot fondue. Naturally the prongs of the fork become very hot, but the plastic or wooden handles remain cool.

Always transfer the hot food from the very hot fondue fork to an ordinary fork before trying to eat it, for the heated metal prongs could burn your mouth.

SERVING DISHES OR DIVIDED PLATES
are not sold as part of a complete fondue set, but these are important to hold the pieces of meat, fish or other dippers.

Arrange the food in as attractive a manner as possible so that your fondue table looks interesting and colourful.

Garnish diced meat, fish, etc with parsley or other salad ingredients.

FONDUE SUCCESS
The success of the fondues depends upon :
1 Careful heating of the ingredients. Check temperature of the oil or sauce carefully.
2 Using good quality oil.
3 Using cheese that cooks well (see the recipes).
4 Keeping the food pleasantly warm or hot over the special heaters.

SAFETY TIPS
Safety techniques similar to those developed in kitchen cooking should be maintained when cooking at the table. Although the possibility of flare-ups or burns is remote, the old adage 'an ounce of prevention is worth a pound of cure' still prevails in this cooking situation.

The important aspect of tabletop cooking is that you should be in complete control of the cooking. A sturdy fondue stand and level table reduce the chances of accidental tipping. Set the fondue unit out of the reach of young children to avoid their quick, unpredictable movements. In fact, fondue is most easily served at an all-adult party.

Keep the fondue heater away from curtains.

If heating oil remember that 1 level teaspoon salt, added to the oil when it reaches the required temperature, lessens the tendency of the oil to spatter.

Should a flare-up develop during dinner, smother the flames quickly by sliding the cover of the fondue pot over the burning area. In addition, a fire extinguisher should be easily accessible to the dining area.

Occasionally a finger may be burned from contact with the hot equipment or hot food. A minor burn can be treated by running cold water over the burn for 15 to 20 minutes, then drying and dressing it with dry gauze. Needless to say, more extensive burns should receive prompt medical attention.

The Buffet Fondue

On this and the next page you will find a menu for a buffet meal. This includes the three fondues, pictured opposite, which can be served as appetizers. These are followed by a simple savoury, fruit, and cake. The quantities given are enough to serve 12-16 people.

```
╔══════════════════════════════╗
║            MENU              ║
║                              ║
║   Cheese and Bean Dunk       ║
║   Sausage-Avocado Dip        ║
║     Hot Shrimp Dip           ║
║  Assorted dippers such as    ║
║ crisps, radishes, and celery ║
║   Turkey Saladwiches         ║
║      Fresh Fruit             ║
║   Coconut Diamonds           ║
║        Drinks                ║
╚══════════════════════════════╝
```

PLAN OF CAMPAIGN

Prepare and bake the Coconut Diamonds, and allow to cool.

Make the filling for the Turkey Saladwiches and keep in a cool place. Scoop the centres out of the rolls ready to toast or bake.

Prepare the ingredients to serve with the three appetizers. Arrange the pieces of celery, radishes, spring onions, carrots, biscuits, crisps, etc on a tray and put the fresh fruit on a dish.

Put all the ingredients for the appetizers into pans and heat over the cooker, then transfer to fondue pots over the three heaters. Candle-type heaters could be used for this menu.

Cheese and Bean Dunk

Cooking time: 8-10 minutes

Chop 3 rashers bacon, 8 spring onions, and 1 clove garlic finely. Fry gently for 3 minutes. Add sieved or emulsified contents of two 15¾ oz (450 gm) cans baked beans in tomato sauce, and 11 oz (310 gm) grated Cheddar cheese.

Heat gently, pour into fondue pot over fondue heater. Top with more chopped spring onions. Makes 2 pints (nearly 1¼ litres).

Sausage-Avocado Dip

Cooking time: 18-20 minutes

8-10 oz (225-285 gm) pork sausages
2 large ripe avocado pears
1 tablespoon lemon juice
6 tablespoons soured cream
2 tablespoons orange juice
¼ teaspoon salt

GARNISH:
1 slice of lemon

Fry sausages gently, skin them, then cut into fine pieces. Drain well on kitchen paper. Halve and skin the avocado pears, remove the stones, and mash.

In a saucepan, combine the avocado pulp with the sausages and the rest of the ingredients. Heat for a few minutes, stirring all the time. Transfer to the fondue pot; place over the burner. Garnish with a lemon twist. Makes 1 pint (generous ½ litre).

Hot Shrimp Dip

Cooking time: 10 minutes

15 oz (425 gm) can cream of scampi or lobster soup
8 oz (225 gm) cream cheese
2 tablespoons thick cream
2 teaspoons lemon juice
1 teaspoon grated horseradish or horse-radish cream
¼ teaspoon Worcestershire sauce

GARNISH:
shrimps or prawns
parsley

Blend the soup and cheese, add the cream, lemon juice, horseradish or horseradish cream, and Worcestershire sauce. Transfer to the fondue pot, and place over the heater. Heat gently, stirring well until the mixture is smooth. Garnish with a few cooked peeled shrimps or prawns, and parsley. Makes 1 pint (generous ½ litre).

Cheese and Bean Dunk (left); Sausage-Avocado Dip (centre) and Hot Shrimp Dip (right).

Turkey Saladwiches

Cooking time: 5 minutes

2 oz (55 gm) almonds, finely chopped
1½ lb (¾ kilo) cooked turkey, diced
8 oz (225 gm) celery, finely diced
1 small onion, finely chopped
1 green pepper, diced
1 red pepper, diced
3 tablespoons lemon juice
½ pint (¼ litre) thick mayonnaise
16 crusty round rolls

Toast the almonds under the grill for 1-2 minutes. Combine all the ingredients except the rolls; chill. Halve and scoop out the centre of each roll to make slight hollows; toast. Fill each half with the cold turkey mixture and serve at once.
Makes 32 savouries.

NB: The halved rolls may be crisped in the oven if preferred, and the cold filling put in. If liked, heat the filling in the top of a double saucepan, and put into the halved rolls.

Coconut Diamonds

Cooking time: 35 minutes

Cream together 6 oz (170 gm) butter or margarine, softened; 4 oz (115 gm) granulated sugar, and ½ teaspoon salt. Stir in 8 oz (225 gm) sieved self-raising flour (or plain flour with 2 level teaspoons baking powder). Divide dough in half. Pat each half onto the bottom of a 9 in (23 cm) square shallow cake tin. Bake just above the centre of a very moderate oven, 325-350°F (170-180°C), Gas No 3, for 15 minutes, or until lightly browned.

Meanwhile, beat 4 eggs lightly; add 2 teaspoons vanilla essence. Gradually add 1 lb (almost ½ kilo) moist brown sugar, beating till just blended. Add 1 oz (30 gm) sieved flour and 1 teaspoon salt. Stir in 6 oz (170 gm) desiccated coconut and 4 oz (115 gm) walnuts, coarsely chopped.

Spread half the coconut mixture over each baked layer. Bake for another 20 minutes or until a skewer comes out clean. Cool. Cut into diamond shapes.
Makes 36-40 diamonds.

Interesting First Courses

The dishes on this and the next page are ideal to serve as an hors d'oeuvre. They are not too filling or strongly flavoured, so you will not spoil your appetite for the courses that follow. A hot 'meal starter' is an excellent choice to serve before a cold salad. Choose one or two recipes only.

Arrange the prepared food, fondue *and* dinner forks on the table, plus small plates and napkins. Heat the oil, *check the temperature* (see page 16), then transfer the oil to the fondue heater. Do not attempt to pre-cook the dishes; the *fun* of fondue eating is for everyone to cook their own food.

Tasty Beef Appetizers

Cooking time: 1-2 minutes

> 3 oz (85 gm) cream cheese, softened
> 1 teaspoon chopped onion, fresh or dried
> 16 oz (455 gm) can sauerkraut, well drained and chopped
> 12 oz (340 gm) can corned beef, flaked
> 1 oz (30 gm) fine dried breadcrumbs
> COATING:
> 2 oz (55 gm) flour
> 6 tablespoons evaporated milk
> 3 oz (85 gm) fine dried breadcrumbs
> FRYING:
> olive or frying oil

Combine the cream cheese and onion. If using dried onion leave to stand for a short time in the cheese so that it becomes moist. Add the sauerkraut, corned beef, and 1 oz (30 gm) of breadcrumbs; mix well. Shape into 1 in (2½ cm) balls. Roll in flour, dip in evaporated milk, then coat in the remaining breadcrumbs. Chill for an hour if possible.

Pour the oil into the fondue pan to no more than half capacity or to a depth of 2 in (5 cm). Heat on the cooker to 375°F (190°C). Transfer the pan to the fondue heater, and put the appetizers into a serving bowl; leave at room temperature. Spear with fondue forks; fry in hot oil until golden. Transfer to dinner forks before eating.
Makes about 100 appetizers.

Crab-Potato Nibblers

Cooking time: 1-2 minutes

Prepare enough instant mashed potato for 2 portions, according to package directions, or cook and mash 4 medium potatoes. Add 1 teaspoon dried or chopped fresh onion to the water in which the potatoes are reconstituted or cooked. Stir in 1¼ teaspoons Worcestershire sauce; ⅛ teaspoon garlic salt; a shake of white pepper, and just enough milk to make a sticky consistency.

Drain and flake the contents of a 7½ oz (215 gm) can crab meat. Blend with the potato mixture. Shape into bite-sized balls; dip into 1 lightly beaten egg, then roll in 2 oz (55 gm) fine dried breadcrumbs. Chill for an hour if possible.

Pour oil into a fondue pan to no more than half capacity or to a depth of 2 inches (5 cm). Heat on the cooker to 375°F (190°C). Transfer the pan to the fondue heater, put the balls into a serving dish, and leave at room temperature. Spear with fondue forks and fry in hot oil until golden.

Makes 36 appetizers.

Cocktail Meatballs

Cooking time: 1-2 minutes

Combine 1 beaten egg; 1½ tablespoons fine dried breadcrumbs; 1 tablespoon finely chopped onion or chives; 2 teaspoons capers, drained; ½ teaspoon salt; ¼ teaspoon dried thyme, and a shake of pepper. Add 8 oz (225 gm) raw minced beef, and mix well. Form into ¾ in (1½ cm) meatballs. Keep cool until ready to fry.

Pour oil into fondue pan to no more than half capacity, or to a depth of 2 in (5 cm). Heat on the cooker to 350°F (180°C). Transfer the pan to the fondue heater. Put meatballs into a serving bowl; leave at room temperature. Spear with fondue forks and fry in hot oil, then dip in selected sauce.

Makes about 60 meatballs.

Suggested sauces: Creamy Ketchup Sauce, Spicy Tomato Sauce, White Mustard Sauce, (pages 25 and 26).

Crispy Vegetable Bites

Cooking time: 2-3 minutes

4 oz (115 gm) fine dried breadcrumbs
1 oz (30 gm) grated Parmesan cheese
1 teaspoon paprika
$\frac{1}{2}$ teaspoon salt
2 eggs, lightly beaten
1 tablespoon water
1 small cauliflower
2 medium carrots
1 aubergine

FRYING:
olive or frying oil

Mix the breadcrumbs, cheese, paprika, and $\frac{1}{4}$ teaspoon salt. Combine the eggs, 1 tablespoon water, and remaining salt. Divide the white part of the cauliflower into bite-sized flowerets. Peel the carrots and aubergine, and cut into thin slices. Dip the vegetables first into the egg, then into the crumb mixture, and repeat.

Pour oil into fondue pan to no more than half capacity or to a depth of 2 in (5 cm). Heat on cooker to 375°F (190°C). Transfer the pan to fondue heater. Put the vegetables into a serving bowl, spear them with fondue forks, and fry in the hot oil.
Serves 6-8.

Shrimp Toast

Cooking time: 1-2 minutes

Finely chop or mince 1 lb ($\frac{1}{2}$ kilo) peeled shrimps or prawns. Add $2\frac{1}{2}$ tablespoons finely chopped onion; 1 egg, beaten; 1 teaspoon flour; 2 teaspoons lemon juice; $\frac{3}{4}$ teaspoon salt, and a shake of pepper. Trim crusts from 6 slices of bread; cut each slice into 4-6 pieces. Spread shrimp mixture on both sides of the bread.

Pour oil into fondue pan to no more than half capacity or to a depth of 2 in (5 cm). Heat on the cooker to 375°F (190°C). Transfer to the fondue heater. Have coated bread at room temperature. Spear with fondue forks; fry in hot oil.
Makes 24-36 appetizers.

Carousel Fondue set. The tray revolves so that your guests can help themselves easily to the various sauces.

Fruity Ham Balls

Cooking time: 2 minutes

8 oz (225 gm) cooked ham, minced
1 oz (30 gm) soft breadcrumbs
4 tablespoons soured cream or fresh thick cream and a squeeze of lemon juice
2 teaspoons finely chopped onion
$\frac{1}{2}$ teaspoon grated horseradish or 1 teaspoon horseradish cream
small can pineapple cubes, well drained and quartered

COATING:
1 egg, beaten
2 oz (55 gm) fine dried breadcrumbs

FRYING:
olive or frying oil

Combine ham, breadcrumbs, soured cream (or cream and lemon juice), onion, and horseradish or horseradish cream; chill well. Shape about 1 teaspoon ham mixture around each pineapple piece. Dip in egg, then in dried breadcrumbs. Allow to stand for about 30 minutes or longer if possible in a cool place.

Pour oil into fondue pan to no more than half capacity or to a depth of 2 in (5 cm). Heat on the cooker to 375°F (190°C). Transfer the pan to the fondue heater. Put the ham balls in a serving bowl at room temperature. Spear with fondue forks; fry in hot oil until golden. Dip in the selected sauce.
Makes about 48 meatballs.
Suggested sauces: Spicy Pineapple Sauce, Horseradish Sauce, Mustard Sauce (pages 24 and 26).

A Wine-tasting Party

Cheese and wine are excellent partners. Any of the cheese fondues (pages 31 to 33) would be an ideal choice for a wine party, or follow the interesting but simple menu suggested below.

MENU

Polka-dot Pinwheels
French-Fried Cheese
Cheese Tray, rolls,
biscuits, butter
Salad   Fresh Fruit
Wines

Wine-tasting for the non-connoisseur should be practical and simple so that guests can learn to identify their preference. Invite only as many guests as can move comfortably around the room and buy only a few wines. See pages 36 and 37 for the Wine Guide.

Polka-dot Pinwheels

No cooking

  1 fresh large white sandwich loaf
  2-3 oz (55-85 gm) butter, softened
  8 oz (225 gm) chicken paste
  1 large red pepper, very finely diced
  ½ teaspoon curry powder
  2 green peppers

Remove the crusts from the bread and cut lengthways into ¼ in (½ cm) thick slices. Spread one side of the bread with butter. Blend the chicken paste, the red pepper, and the curry powder.

Spread the buttered side of each slice with 2 tablespoons of the filling. Cut the flesh of the green peppers into thin strips. Place 5 strips an equal distance apart on top of the filling. Roll each slice of bread firmly (like a Swiss roll). Wrap in foil or clear plastic wrap, and chill for 1 hour. Cut into ⅜ in (¾ cm) slices. Makes about 40 pinwheels.

French Fried Cheese

Cooking time: ½ minute

  approximately 1½ lb (¾ kilo) assorted cheeses
  2 eggs, beaten
  3 oz (85 gm) fine dried breadcrumbs

FRYING:
  olive or frying oil

In this recipe use soft cheeses with a crust (Camembert or Brie), semi-hard (Bel Paese or processed cheese) or hard (Cheddar, Gruyère, Edam and Gouda) cheeses.

Cut the cheeses into ½ in (1 cm) squares. For soft cheeses, shape crust around soft centre as much as possible. Dip in egg, then in breadcrumbs; repeat for a second time. (A thick coating prevents the cheese leaking through the egg and crumbs.)

Pour the oil into the fondue pan to no more than half capacity or a depth of 2 in (5 cm). Heat on cooker to 375°F (190°C). Transfer pan to the fondue heater. Spear cheese with fondue forks; fry in the hot oil for ½ minute only. Cool slightly before eating.

Serves 6-8 as separate savoury or 12-16 as part of this menu.

Cheese Tray

Choose a variety of cheeses, including:
Hard cheese   Cheddar plus one other, such as Cheshire, Lancashire, Double Gloucester.
Soft cheese   Brie, Camembert, etc.
Veined cheese   Stilton, Gorganzola or Roquefort, Danish Blue, or similar.
Lesser known cheeses   Tôme de Raisin (cheese coated with grape pips), Sage Derby (flavoured with a ribbon of sage).

Serve with rolls and biscuits, radish roses, celery and bunches of grapes.

French Fried Cheese provides a delicious snack with wine. The crisp outside is a pleasing contrast to the creamy centre. Seen here accompanied by Polka-dot Pinwheels.

Cooking Meat and Fish

Dinner is easy on the hostess when the main dish is a meat or fish fondue. The hostess sets the table and the guests do the rest themselves.

The traditional fondue recipe in this section is Beef Fondue. Although also called Fondue Bourguignonne (Burgundian Fondue), its connection with Burgundy (a region of France) or Burgundy wine is obscure. Beef Fondue consists of cubes of tender beef cooked in hot oil and then dipped in a piquant sauce. Similar fondues substitute other meat or fish for beef.

Amounts to allow: When planning a fondue meal, allow 8 oz (225 gm) trimmed uncooked meat or skinned fish per person if this is to be the main dish, or less, of course, if you have a selection of other fondues or dishes in the menu.

Equipment needed: Provide a fondue fork per person if possible and one fondue pan for 4-6 persons. If you have insufficient fondue forks you could use long wooden skewers or kebab skewers, but remember that ordinary metal skewers (without insulated ends) would become unbearably hot if put into the hot oil.

In addition have dinner forks so that the *very hot* food may be transferred to these. You will need plates, napkins and dishes of sauce (see pages 7 to 9). *Make quite certain* the fondue pan of hot oil is in a safe place and on a metal tray so the high temperature does not mark the table. (See page 9 for safety hints.)

Choosing the menu: A meat or fish fondue with a sauce or a selection of sauces needs an interesting vegetable or salad as an accompaniment, crusty rolls or bread, a light refreshing dessert, and wine to provide a first class meal.

Preparing the food: Cut the meat or fish into bite-sized pieces about 1 hour before the meal, and leave them at room temperature; if they are too cold they take too long to heat and cook. Cover the dishes until the last minute, so the outside of the meat or fish does not become hard looking and dry. Arrange the salad and accompaniments on the table and measure the oil into the fondue heater. Do not put this onto the cooker too early.

Choice of oil: Choose a really first class frying oil—there is a good selection available. Olive oil is an excellent oil, but it does have a more definite flavour than some others, which tends to be 'carried over' to the meat or fish. It also smokes more readily than some oils. If you are particularly fond of the taste of butter then use it mixed with oil. All butter darkens and burns rather easily for fondue cooking so use one part butter to three parts oil. The butter should be clarified before using. To do this, melt the butter over a low heat and allow to cool; then pour off the top layer for the fondue, and discard the bottom layer. The use of some butter gives a richer flavour to the meat or fish.

Method of heating: If you have a very efficient fondue heater, and if you allow sufficient time, you could use it to bring the oil to the right temperature. However, it is generally wiser and certainly quicker to heat the oil on the cooker. When it reaches the right temperature, add a level teaspoon of salt to minimize splashing and carry *very carefully* to the fondue heater.
Never over-fill the fondue pan with oil; it should be half filled or filled to a depth of 2 in (5 cm).

Testing the temperature of the oil: A thermometer is not an expensive item and it does ensure that the oil is just the right temperature for cooking the particular mixture or food. It is possible to test the oil by dropping in a portion of the food and timing the cooking. If it takes longer than the time given in the recipe, heat the oil a little more on the cooker, then test again. If the food cooks too quickly, allow the oil to cool before carrying to the heater. If preferred, use a cube of day-old bread. Drop this into the very hot oil. If it turns golden brown within about 50-60 seconds the temperature is 350°F (180°C); if it turns golden brown within about 20-25 seconds it is 375°F (190°C); and if it turns brown at once it is 400-425°F (up to 220°C). This is *very* hot so be careful.

Jazzy Beef Bites

Cooking time: 1½-2 minutes

1 tablespoon tomato ketchup
1 teaspoon grated horseradish or horseradish cream
1 teaspoon prepared mustard
½ teaspoon chopped onion, dried or
fresh
½ teaspoon salt
shake of pepper
8 oz (225 gm) minced beef
½ oz (15 gm) fine soft breadcrumbs
4 oz (115 gm) Cheddar cheese
FRYING:
olive or frying oil

Combine tomato ketchup, horseradish or horse-radish cream, mustard, onion, salt and pepper; allow to stand for 10 minutes, then add the minced beef and breadcrumbs. Cut the cheese into ¼ in (½ cm) cubes. Shape the meat mixture around the cheese to form ¾ in (1½ cm) balls. Spear on wooden skewers or fine metal skewers (the mixture is a little 'crumbly' for fondue forks) and put onto flat plates.

Pour the oil into the fondue pan to no more than half capacity or to a depth of 2 in (5 cm). Heat on cooker to 375°F (190°C). Transfer the pan to the fondue heater. Fry the meatballs in the hot oil.
Makes about 30 meatballs.

Beef Fondue

Cooking time: 2-4 minutes

1½ lb (¾ kilo) fillet, rump or lean sirloin
   steak
FRYING:
olive or frying oil

Cut the meat into ¾ in (1½ cm) cubes. Pour the oil into the fondue pan to no more than half capacity or to a depth of 2 in (5 cm). Heat on the cooker to 425°F (220°C). Transfer the pan to the fondue heater. Put the beef into an attractive dish at room temperature. Spear the meat with fondue forks, and fry in hot oil until cooked to taste. Dip into the selected sauce.
Serves 4.
Suggested sauces: Bordelaise Sauce, Caper Sauce, Garlic Butter, Green Goddess Sauce, Horseradish Sauce, Mushroom Sauce, Olive Sauce, Wine Sauce (pages 23 to 29).

This is a Beef Fondue (Beef Bourguignonne) set but it is equally suitable for all meat and fish fondues. The picture shows a sectioned tray to hold pieces of food.

Fondued Sirloin Steak

Cooking time: 1-2 minutes

Cut 1 lb (½ kilo) sirloin steak into very thin 3×1 in (7×2 cm) strips. Combine 6 table-spoons salad oil; 6 tablespoons red wine; 1½ tablespoons tomato ketchup; 1½ tablespoons black treacle; 2 tablespoons finely chopped crystallized ginger; 1 clove garlic, crushed; ½ teaspoon salt; ½ teaspoon curry powder and a shake of pepper.

Pour marinade over steak and leave for 2 hours at room temperature. Drain well; pat dry with absorbent paper. Thread onto wooden or metal kebab skewers, accordian style.

Pour the oil into the fondue pan to no more than half capacity or to a depth of 2 in (5 cm). Heat on cooker to 425°F (220°C). Transfer the pan to the fondue heater. Have skewered meat strips at room temperature on a serving plate. Fry in hot oil for 1-2 minutes, or until cooked to taste.
Serves 4.

When heating oil for fondue, it is advisable to use a thermometer to assure that the specified temperature has been reached. Do not allow the oil to smoke.

Sausage Meatballs

Cooking time: 10 minutes

12 oz (340 gm) pork sausagemeat
1 medium onion, finely chopped
16 oz (455 gm) can sauerkraut
½ oz (15 gm) soft fine breadcrumbs
3 oz (85 gm) creamed cheese
2 tablespoons chopped parsley
1 teaspoon prepared mustard
¼ teaspoon garlic salt
⅛ teaspoon pepper

COATING:
1 oz (30 gm) flour
2 eggs, well beaten
3 tablespoons milk
3 oz (85 gm) fine dried breadcrumbs

FRYING:
olive or frying oil

Blend the sausagemeat with the chopped onion, and form into a flat layer. Put into a frying pan and brown for a few minutes on either side. Drain on absorbent paper, then chop finely and mix with the well drained and chopped sauerkraut and breadcrumbs.

Combine the softened creamed cheese, chopped parsley, mustard, salt and pepper. Stir into sauerkraut mixture; chill. Shape meat mixture into ¾ in (1½ cm) balls, and coat with flour. Combine the well beaten eggs and milk. Roll balls in the egg mixture, then in breadcrumbs.

Pour oil into fondue pan to no more than half capacity or to a depth of 2 in (5 cm). Heat on cooker to 375°F (190°C). Transfer the pan to the fondue heater. Have meatballs at room temperature. Spear meatballs with fondue forks; fry in hot oil for ½-1 minute, or until golden. Dip into the selected sauce.
Makes 60 meatballs.
Suggested sauces: Sweet-sour Sauce, Mustard Sauce, Curry Sauce, Creamy Ketchup Sauce (pages 25 to 29).

Fondue Italiano

Cooking time: 40 minutes

2 oz (55 gm) mushrooms
1 onion
1 clove garlic
2 tablespoons olive oil
15 oz (425 gm) can tomatoes
  (preferably Italian 'plum type')
½ lb (225 gm) minced beef
1 tablespoon cornflour
pinch of dried oregano (wild marjoram)
6 tablespoons red wine, preferably Chianti
12 oz (340 gm) Cheddar or Gruyère cheese, grated
4 oz (115 gm) Mozzarella cheese, finely chopped

Chop the mushrooms and onion, and crush the clove of garlic. Heat the oil in a pan, then add the vegetables, and cook for 3 minutes. Stir in the tomatoes and liquid from the can, and heat gently. Add the meat and simmer for 30 minutes, stirring from time to time. Keep the pan covered so that the liquid does not evaporate. Blend together the cornflour, oregano, and Chianti; add to the meat mixture. Cook, stirring until thickened. Remove from the heat, add the cheeses gradually, allow these to melt but *do not* continue cooking.

Transfer to the fondue pot; place over heater. Spear 'dippers' with fondue forks; dip into the mixture, swirling to coat. (If fondue becomes thick, add a little warmed Chianti.)
Serves about 6.
Suggested dippers: cubes of bread, cooked Jerusalem artichokes or new potatoes, cooked cannelloni (large tube-like pasta).
NB: ½ packet of spaghetti sauce mix could be used instead of mushrooms, onion, garlic and oil, and tomato sauce substituted for canned tomatoes.

Filled Lamb Balls

Curry subtly flavours the meat

Cooking time: 2 minutes

  8 oz (225 gm) minced lamb
  1 tablespoon fine dried breadcrumbs
  1 teaspoon finely chopped spring onion
    or tops of chives
  ¼ teaspoon salt
  ¼ teaspoon curry powder
  3 oz (85 gm) Gruyère cheese

FRYING:
  olive or frying oil

Combine the lamb, breadcrumbs, onion or chives, salt, and curry powder. Cut the cheese into ½ in (1 cm) cubes. Shape about 1 teaspoon meat mixture around each cheese cube.
  Pour the oil into the fondue pan to no more than half capacity or to a depth of 2 in (5 cm). Heat on the cooker to 375°F (190°C). Transfer the pan to the fondue heater. Have lamb balls at room temperature in a serving bowl. Spear lamb balls with fondue forks; fry in hot oil for about 2 minutes, or until browned.

Makes about 32 meatballs.

Pork or Ham Fondue

Cooking time: 1-3 minutes

  2 lb (1 kilo) pork fillet or lean gammon
    or 1½ lb (¾ kilo) cooked ham

FRYING:
  olive or frying oil

Cut the meat into ¾ in (1½ cm) cubes. Pour the oil into fondue pan to no more than half capacity or to a depth of 2 in (5 cm). Heat on the cooker to 425°F (220°C). Transfer the pan to the fondue heater. Have meat at room temperature in a serving dish. Spear meat with fondue forks; fry the uncooked pork or gammon in hot oil for 2-3 minutes, but allow 1 minute only for cooked ham. Dip in selected sauce.

Serves 4.

Suggested sauces: Onion Sauce, Marmalade Sauce, Herb Butter, Mustard Sauce (pages 24 to 29).

Chicken Fondue

Cooking time: 2-3 minutes

  2 lb (1 kilo) chicken breasts

FRYING:
  olive or frying oil

Skin the chicken breasts, remove the bones, and cut the meat into ¾ in (1½ cm) cubes. Pour the oil into the fondue pan to no more than half capacity or to a depth of 2 inches (5 cm). Heat on cooker to 425°F (220°C). Transfer the pan to the fondue heater. Have chicken cubes at room temperature in serving bowl. Spear cubes with fondue forks; fry in hot oil for 2-3 minutes. Transfer to dinner forks; dip in selected sauce.

Serves 4.

Suggested sauces: Béarnaise Sauce, Tangy Cranberry Sauce, 1-2-3 Sauce, Creamy Curry Sauce (pages 23 to 28).

NB: Very lean breast of duck could be used instead of chicken.

Bacon-wrapped Chicken

Cooking time: 1-2 minutes

Skin, bone, and cut the breasts from 2 young frying chickens into ¾ in (1½ cm) cubes. If using frozen chickens, allow to defrost. Combine 3 tablespoons Soy sauce, 1½ tablespoons dry sherry, ½ oz (15 gm) sugar, 1 tablespoon vinegar and ¼ teaspoon ground ginger; mix well. Add the chicken cubes; allow to stand for 30 minutes at room temperature, turning occasionally. Drain well.
  Cut each of 6 long rashers streaky bacon in thirds crosswise, then in half lengthwise (36 pieces). Wrap one piece around each cube of chicken, securing with a wooden cocktail stick. Chill thoroughly, at least 1 hour before cooking.
  Pour oil into fondue pan to no more than half capacity or to a depth of 2 in (5 cm). Heat on the cooker to 375°F (190°C). Transfer pan to the fondue heater. Have meat at room temperature on a serving plate. Fry chicken cubes in hot oil for 1-2 minutes or until the bacon is cooked.

Makes 36 appetizers.

Veal Strips

Cooking time: 2 minutes

Pound 1½ lb (¾ kilo) veal cutlet to about ⅛ in (¼ cm) thick. Cut into 3 × 1 in (7 × 2 cm) strips. Combine about 1 oz (30 gm) flour and ¼ teaspoon salt. Coat veal strips with flour mixture, dip in 2 beaten eggs, then in 2 oz (55 gm) fine dried breadcrumbs. Loosely thread each strip on wooden or metal kebab skewers, accordian style.

Pour oil into the fondue pan to no more than half capacity or to a depth of 2 in (5 cm). Heat on cooker to 425°F (220°C). Transfer the pan to the fondue heater. Have skewered veal at room temperature on a serving plate. Fry in the hot oil for about 2 minutes. Dip in selected sauce.

Serves 4.

Suggested sauces: Bordelaise Sauce, Anchovy Butter, Spicy Tomato Sauce, Garlic Butter (pages 25 to 29).

Spicy Appetizer Meatballs

Cooking time: 20 minutes

- 1 oz (30 gm) fine dried breadcrumbs
- 1 egg, lightly beaten
- 1 teaspoon prepared mustard
- ½ teaspoon salt
- shake of pepper
- 12 oz (340 gm) minced beef
- 4 oz (115 gm) can, tube or jar liver paste or pâté

COATING:
- 2-3 oz (55-85 gm) cornflakes

Blend the ingredients for the meatballs together. Shape into 1 in (2 cm) meatballs, using a rounded teaspoon of meat mixture for each. Roll in the crushed cornflakes, and refrigerate overnight.

Cook on a greased shallow baking tray towards the top of a very moderate oven, 350°F (180°C), Gas Mark 4, for 10 minutes. Turn gently with a spoon, and continue cooking for a further 10 minutes.

Makes about 60 meatballs.

Fish and Seafood Fondue

Cooking time: 2 minutes

- 8 oz (225 gm) white fish fillets (free from skin and bone)
- 1 medium lobster
- 8 oz (225 gm) peeled prawns

FRYING:
- olive or frying oil

Cut the uncooked fish, lobster meat, and prawns into bite-sized pieces; pat dry with kitchen paper. Pour the oil into the fondue pan to no more than half capacity or to a depth of 2 in (5 cm). Heat on the cooker to 375°F (190°C). Transfer the pan to the fondue heater. Have the fish and seafood at room temperature in a serving dish.

Spear the fish with fondue forks, fry in the hot oil till lightly browned. Dip into the selected sauce.
Serves 4.

Suggested sauces: Caper Sauce, Cocktail Sauce, Dill Sauce. Sauce à la Relish, Sweet-sour Sauce, Tartare Sauce (pages 23 to 29). See picture page 22.

NB: Some fish such as crabs, oysters and scallops are not well suited for fondue.

Fish Balls

Cooking time: 15 minutes

- 1 lb (½ kilo) white fish, weighed without bones and skin
- 1 oz (30 gm) butter
- 2 tablespoons milk
- seasoning
- 2 oz (55 gm) soft breadcrumbs

COATING:
- 2 eggs, beaten
- 2 oz (55 gm) crisp breadcrumbs

Cook the fish with the butter, milk, and seasoning on a covered dish over a pan of boiling water. Flake or mince the fish finely, mix with the liquid from the dish and the crumbs. Cool, then form into small balls. Coat with beaten eggs and crumbs. Cook and serve as Fish and Seafood Fondue above.
Makes about 36 Fish Balls.

Sauces for Fondues

MAKING SAUCES

Most meat, poultry and fish fondues need a sauce or dip to add interest to the food. Here are some interesting suggestions. Remember:

1 When sauces are thickened by boiling or simmering, you *must* stir to keep the mixture smooth and to prevent it from burning.
2 The metric equivalent given of $\frac{1}{4}$ litre = $\frac{1}{2}$ pint is a practical rounded off conversion. Be rather generous when measuring the $\frac{1}{4}$ litre of liquid to give the right consistency.
3 If you wish to keep sauces thickened with flour or cornflour hot for any length of time, put *damp* greaseproof paper over the sauce to prevent a skin forming on top. If the sauce forms a skin or becomes slightly lumpy, whisk sharply or emulsify in the liquidizer (blender) goblet.

CHOICE OF SAUCES

Serve a variety of sauces with fondues. Choose one from each group, ie bland; fruit; vegetable; hot; salty, or sharp sauces.

BLAND FLAVOURED SAUCES

The following sauces and dips are comparatively mild in flavour, and blend well with all types of food and with other sauces.

Uncooked Caper Sauce

Blend $\frac{1}{2}$ pint ($\frac{1}{4}$ litre) mayonnaise or salad cream with 1 tablespoon capers plus 2 teaspoons liquid from the bottle.
Makes $\frac{1}{2}$ pint ($\frac{1}{4}$ litre).

Spear pieces of salmon, prawns, or other fish, and heat fondue style (see page 21).

Béarnaise Sauce

Time to thicken: 8-10 minutes

Combine 2 tablespoons tarragon vinegar; 1 teaspoon *finely* chopped shallot or onion; 4 whole peppercorns, crushed; and bouquet garni*. Simmer until the vinegar is reduced by half. Strain; add 1 tablespoon cold water.

Beat 4 egg yolks in the top of a double saucepan or basin over hot, but *not* boiling water until thick and creamy. Slowly add herb liquid. Have 4 oz (115 gm) butter at room temperature. Add the butter very gradually to the egg yolks. Stir until all the butter has been used and the sauce is as smooth as thick cream. Remove from heat, add salt and pepper to taste, and 1 teaspoon chopped fresh tarragon or $\frac{1}{4}$ teaspoon dried tarragon leaves, crushed.
Makes $\frac{1}{2}$ pint ($\frac{1}{4}$ litre).

*Bouquet garni—a selection of fresh herbs tied in a small bunch with cotton. They generally include a bay leaf, thyme, parsley, rosemary, tarragon (or marjoram) or other herbs.

Caper Sauce

Cooking time: 10 minutes

Make a white sauce with 1 oz (30 gm) butter or margarine; 1 oz (30 gm) flour and $\frac{1}{2}$ pint ($\frac{1}{4}$ litre) milk. When thickened add $\frac{1}{2}$-1 tablespoon capers plus a little liquid from the bottle, and 1-2 tablespoons thick cream. Do not allow to boil after adding the capers, etc.
Makes $\frac{1}{2}$ pint ($\frac{1}{4}$ litre).

Dill Sauce

No cooking

Combine $\frac{1}{2}$ pint ($\frac{1}{4}$ litre) soured cream; 1 tablespoon chopped chives (or use the green tops of spring onions); 1 teaspoon vinegar; $\frac{1}{2}$ teaspoon finely chopped onion; 2 teaspoons finely chopped dill (or $\frac{1}{2}$ teaspoon dried dill), and $\frac{1}{4}$ teaspoon salt. Mix well.
Makes $\frac{1}{2}$ pint ($\frac{1}{4}$ litre).

Mayonnaise Based Sauces

All quantities are based on ¼ pint (140 ml) of thick mayonnaise, and serve 4-5.

A Sauce Marie Rose: Add 2 tablespoons tomato ketchup; 2 tablespoons thick cream, and 1 tablespoon sherry.

B Piquant Tartare Sauce: Add 1 tablespoon chopped vinegar pickle; ½-1 tablespoon chopped parsley; 1-2 teaspoons chopped raw or canned red pepper, and 1 teaspoon grated or chopped onion.

C Tartare Sauce: Add ½-1 tablespoon chopped gherkins; ½-1 tablespoon chopped parsley and ¼-½ tablespoon chopped capers.

FRUIT AND VEGETABLE SAUCES

These sauces are excellent with fondues for they give a refreshing 'bite' to the cooked food.

Spicy Pineapple Sauce

Cooking time: 5 minutes

¼ pint (140 ml) water
1 beef bouillon cube
13¼ oz (375 gm) can crushed pineapple, undrained
3 gingernut biscuits
1½ tablespoons vinegar
shake of pepper
pinch of ground cloves

Boil the water in a saucepan. Dissolve the bouillon cube in the water. Emulsify the remaining ingredients in a liquidizer for 30 seconds. Add to the liquid, and cook, stirring over a low heat until thick.
Makes ¾ pint (425 ml).

Fruit Purées

No cooking

Sieve or emulsify canned or cooked apricots or peaches to give a thick purée. Add a little spice and lemon juice.

Tangy Cranberry Sauce

Cooking time: 15 minutes

1 lb (½ kilo) cranberries
¼ pint (140 ml) water
3 tablespoons brown sugar
1 level tablespoon cornflour
6 tablespoons orange juice
¼ teaspoon ground cinnamon

Put the cranberries, water, and sugar into a saucepan, and simmer until the fruit is *just* tender. Blend the cornflour with the orange juice. Add to the cranberries with the cinnamon, and stir over a low heat until thickened.
Makes about ¾ pint (425 ml).
NB: If using canned cranberry sauce add ½-1 tablespoon sugar only, and omit the water.

Onion Sauces

Onion flavoured sauces and dips are ideal to serve with meat or poultry fondues. Only the sweet and sour sauce is cooked.

A Onion Cheese Sauce: Blend together ½ pint (285 ml) soured cream, and 2 tablespoons dried onion soup mix. Crumble 3 oz (85 gm) Danish blue cheese, and chop 1½ oz (45 gm) walnuts. Blend with the onion mixture. Chill. Makes generous ¾ pint (425 ml).

B Onion Dip: Combine 6 tablespoons soured cream; 1 envelope green onion dip mix; ½ teaspoon Worcestershire sauce, and 2-3 drops Tabasco sauce. Chill thoroughly. Makes ¼ pint (140 ml).

C Sweet-sour Onion Sauce: Melt 1 oz (30 gm) butter with ½ oz (15 gm) sugar over a low heat, stirring until the mixture turns golden; this will take about 5 minutes. Chop 2 medium-sized onions very finely, add to the sugar mixture, and cook for 2 minutes more. Blend in ¾ oz (25 gm) flour; add ½ pint (¼ litre) beef stock (or use water with a beef bouillon cube). Cook, stirring until thickened and smooth. Add ½ tablespoon white or brown malt vinegar. Reduce the heat, and simmer the sauce for another 5 minutes. Serve hot.
Makes ½ pint (¼ litre).

Marmalade Sauce

Cooking time: 6-8 minutes

Put 6 tablespoons orange marmalade; 1 tablespoon Soy sauce; a good pinch of garlic salt, and a pinch of ground ginger into a saucepan; bring to the boil. Blend 1 level tablespoon cornflour with 6 tablespoons cold water. Blend with the hot mixture, and stir until thickened and smooth. Add 2 tablespoons lemon juice. Makes $\frac{1}{2}$ pint ($\frac{1}{4}$ litre).

Mushroom Sauces

Mushroom sauces are excellent accompaniments to most fondues. All the recipes need cooking.

A Beef and Mushroom Sauce: Drain one 3 oz (85 gm) can mushrooms, and chop mushrooms. Dissolve 1 beef bouillon cube in $\frac{1}{4}$ pint (140 ml) mushroom liquid and water. Melt 1 oz (30 gm) butter or margarine in a saucepan. Blend in $\frac{1}{2}$ oz (15 gm) flour. Add the beef liquid and cook steadily, stirring until mixture thickens. Lower the heat, add 6 tablespoons soured cream, the mushrooms, and $\frac{1}{2}$-1 tablespoon Worcestershire sauce; heat gently. Makes $\frac{1}{2}$ pint ($\frac{1}{4}$ litre).

B Bordelaise Sauce: Fry 6 oz (170 gm) mushrooms, thinly sliced, in 2 oz (55 gm) butter or margarine until tender. Add 1 oz (30 gm) flour, blended with $\frac{1}{2}$ pint ($\frac{1}{4}$ litre) beef stock; 1 tablespoon red wine, and 1 tablespoon lemon juice. Stir until thickened, add $\frac{1}{2}$-1 teaspoon chopped fresh tarragon, salt and pepper. Makes $\frac{3}{4}$ pint (425 ml).

C Creamy Mushroom Sauce: Heat a $10\frac{1}{2}$ oz (300 gm) can condensed cream of mushroom soup with 6 tablespoons soured cream. Makes 1 pint ($\frac{1}{2}$ litre).

D Wine and Mushroom Sauce: Chop 6 oz (170 gm) mushrooms and 2 medium onions. Fry in 2 oz (55 gm) butter or margarine until just tender. Stir in 1 level tablespoon cornflour; blend in $\frac{3}{4}$ pint (425 ml) red Burgundy and water (proportions to personal taste); 2 tablespoons chopped parsley; salt and pepper. Cook, stirring until mixture thickens. Makes $\frac{3}{4}$ pint (425 ml).

Tomato Sauces

Canned tomato sauce is available, and this may be used as a basis for various flavourings. Although fresh tomatoes are given in some of the recipes below, canned tomatoes could be used. Drain, and use the liquid from the can in a soup or stew.

All recipes make approximately $\frac{1}{2}$ pint ($\frac{1}{4}$ litre). Only sauce B is cooked.

A Creamy Ketchup Sauce: Cream 3 oz (85 gm), cream cheese, softened, then blend in 3 tablespoons soured cream; $1\frac{1}{2}$ tablespoons tomato ketchup; $\frac{1}{4}$ teaspoon salt; $\frac{1}{4}$ teaspoon Worcestershire sauce, and a dash of Tabasco sauce; mix well. Stir in $1\frac{1}{2}$ tablespoons finely chopped green pepper.

B Mexican Hot Sauce: Chop and sieve or emulsify enough tomatoes (about 4-5) to give $\frac{1}{2}$ pint ($\frac{1}{4}$ litre) purée. Put into a saucepan with 3 tablespoons chopped onion; 2 tablespoons vinegar; 1 tablespoon olive oil; 1 teaspoon brown sugar; 1 clove garlic, crushed; $\frac{1}{4}$ teaspoon salt; $\frac{1}{4}$ teaspoon dry mustard, and $\frac{1}{4}$ teaspoon Tabasco sauce. Bring to the boil, add $\frac{1}{2}$-1 teaspoon chilli powder (or more if you like a hot flavour), and simmer for 10 minutes, stirring occasionally. Serve hot or cold.

C Red Sauce: Combine 4 tablespoons tomato ketchup; 2 tablespoons concentrated tomato purée (from a tube or can); $\frac{1}{4}$ pint (140 ml) fresh or canned tomato purée; 2 teaspoons Soy sauce, and a few drops of Tabasco sauce; mix well, and add a pinch of salt and sugar. Chill.

D Spicy Tomato Sauce: Blend $\frac{1}{4}$ pint (140 ml) thick tomato purée; 6 tablespoons soured cream; 2 tablespoons mayonnaise; $\frac{1}{2}$ teaspoon grated fresh horseradish; $\frac{1}{2}$ teaspoon celery salt; a pinch of salt; a little grated nutmeg; $\frac{1}{4}$ teaspoon ground cinnamon and a shake of pepper. Chill.

E 1-2-3 Sauce: Blend about 12 tablespoons tomato ketchup with 2-3 tablespoons vinegar, and a little crushed garlic or garlic salt. Chill thoroughly.

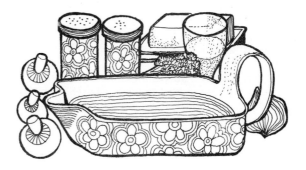

HOT SAUCES

These sauces are all hot in taste. This flavour is given by chilli sauce or powder, curry powder, mustard or horseradish. Add these slowly, *tasting as you do so,* as personal tastes vary considerably.

Horseradish Sauces

The 'bite' of horseradish produces an excellent flavour to serve with fondues. When fresh horseradish is not available, use the bottled variety which is quite moist.

All sauces make approximately $\frac{1}{2}$ pint ($\frac{1}{4}$ litre). Only sauce D is cooked.

A Cocktail Sauce: Blend 2 tablespoons finely grated fresh horseradish; 2 tablespoons lemon juice; 2 teaspoons Worcestershire sauce; 1 teaspoon grated or finely chopped onion, and 12 tablespoons mayonnaise. Add a few drops of chilli sauce.

B Horseradish and Cheese Dip: Beat 8 oz (225 gm) softened cream cheese and $1\frac{1}{2}$-2 tablespoons finely grated fresh horseradish until fluffy. Blend in $1\frac{1}{2}$ tablespoons milk. Chill.

C Horseradish Cream: Fold 2 tablespoons finely grated fresh horseradish into 6 table-spoons thick cream. Add $\frac{1}{2}$ teaspoon salt; a good pinch of sugar; a pinch of dried mustard, and a squeeze of lemon juice. Beat well until thickened.

D Savoury Horseradish Sauce: Melt $1\frac{1}{2}$ oz (45 gm) butter or margarine, and blend in 1 oz (30 gm) flour. Add 3 tablespoons vinegar; $\frac{1}{4}$ pint (140 ml) beef stock; 3 tablespoons finely grated fresh horseradish; 1-2 teaspoons made mustard, and 2 tablespoons brown sugar. Cook slowly, stirring constantly, until thickened. Blend 3 tablespoons beef stock with 1 lightly beaten egg yolk; whisk into the hot sauce, return to the heat, and cook gently without boiling, stirring constantly, until the mixture coats the back of a wooden spoon. Serve hot.

E Soured Horseradish Sauce: Combine $\frac{1}{2}$ pint ($\frac{1}{4}$ litre) soured cream; 2 tablespoons finely grated fresh horseradish; $\frac{1}{4}$ teaspoon salt and a dash of paprika. Chill.

Chilli-Cheese Sauce

Cooking time: 8-10 minutes

8 oz (225 gm) can tomatoes
8 oz (225 gm) processed or Cheddar cheese, shredded or grated
1 fresh red chilli pepper
pinch of salt

Drain the tomatoes, reserving the juice. Chop the tomatoes into small pieces, add the cheese, finely chopped chilli, and 4 tablespoons of the reserved juice. Heat slowly, stirring well, until the cheese melts; add the salt. Serve warm. (If mixture becomes too thick, stir in a little tomato juice.)
Makes scant $\frac{3}{4}$ pint (425 ml).
NB: Chilli peppers are very hot.

Mustard Sauces

These are good with all fondues. Choose French or English mustard.

All sauces make approximately $\frac{1}{2}$ pint ($\frac{1}{4}$ litre). Only sauce C is cooked, while A is heated.

A Creamy Mustard Dip: Combine 2 egg yolks, beaten; $\frac{1}{2}$ oz (15 gm) sugar; 2 table-spoons prepared mustard; $1\frac{1}{2}$ tablespoons vinegar; 1 tablespoon water; $\frac{1}{2}$ oz (15 gm) softened butter; 1 teaspoon finely grated horseradish (or 2 teaspoons horseradish cream) and $\frac{1}{4}$ teaspoon salt in the top of a double saucepan; mix well. Place over boiling water, cook, stirring until thickened, about 2 minutes. Remove from the heat. Stir vigorously, if necessary, until the sauce is smooth. Cool. Fold in 6 tablespoons thick cream, whipped; refrigerate.

B Rémoulade Sauce: Blend $\frac{1}{2}$ pint ($\frac{1}{4}$ litre) mayonnaise with $\frac{1}{2}$-1 tablespoon prepared mustard. Finely chopped parsley could be added if wished.

C White Mustard Sauce: Melt 1 oz (30 gm) butter or margarine in a saucepan. Blend in $\frac{3}{4}$ oz (25 gm) flour; a pinch of salt and white pepper. Stir in $\frac{1}{2}$ pint ($\frac{1}{4}$ litre) milk, then cook steadily, stirring until the mixture thickens. Remove from the heat. Add 1-$1\frac{1}{2}$ tablespoons prepared mustard; mix well. Serve hot.

Mexi-Meatballs (recipe page 34) are cooked in hot oil, then served with Creamy Avocado Sauce (below); Chilli-Cheese Sauce (page 26) and Mexican Hot Sauce (page 25).

Indian Curry Dip

Hot, tangy dip, delicious with meat, poultry or fish.

Cooking time: 10-12 minutes

In a saucepan melt 1 oz (30 gm) butter. Add 1-2 teaspoons curry powder; 1 clove garlic, crushed, or garlic salt, and a pinch of salt; mix well. Blend 2 level tablespoons cornflour with $\frac{1}{2}$ pint ($\frac{1}{4}$ litre) chicken stock (or canned consommé, or water and chicken bouillon cube); add to butter mixture. Cook, stirring until thickened. Pour into the fondue pot on the fondue heater.

Stir in 3 tablespoons tomato ketchup; add 6 tablespoons soured cream. Heat gently. Serve hot as a dip with diced cooked turkey or chicken cubes, cooked prawns, shrimps, or fish balls.

Makes generous $\frac{3}{4}$ pint (425 ml).

Creamy Avocado Sauce

Cooking time: 5-7 minutes

4 rashers bacon
2 medium avocado pears
6 tablespoons soured cream
2 teaspoons lemon juice
$\frac{1}{2}$ teaspoon grated or finely chopped onion
$\frac{1}{4}$ teaspoon salt
good pinch of chilli powder (this is very hot)

Fry the rashers of bacon until crisp, then chop or crumble. Halve and skin the pears, remove the stones, and mash the pulp with the rest of the ingredients. Blend with most of the bacon. Put into the dish, and garnish with the remaining bacon.

Makes generous $\frac{1}{2}$ pint ($\frac{1}{4}$ litre).

Creamy Curry Sauce

Cooking time: 10 minutes

1½ oz (45 gm) butter or margarine
1 teaspoon curry powder
½ oz (15 gm) flour
¼ level teaspoon salt
shake of pepper
scant ½ pint (¼ litre) milk

Melt the butter or margarine. Stir in the curry powder, flour, salt, and pepper. Cook for 2 minutes, stirring all the time. Add the milk and bring to the boil, then stir until thickened. Serve hot.
Makes scant ½ pint (¼ litre).
NB: 1-2 tablespoons thick cream can be added to the sauce when thickened.

Speedy Curry Sauce

No cooking

Blend ½ pint (¼ litre) thick mayonnaise or salad dressing with 1-2 teaspoons curry powder. Add a few sultanas and 1-2 teaspoons sweet chutney if desired.
Makes ½ pint (¼ litre).

Ginger Soy

Cooking time: few minutes

Blend 6 tablespoons Soy sauce and 1½ teaspoons ground ginger in a saucepan. Bring to the boil. Serve hot or cold.
Makes scant ¼ pint (140 ml).

Sauce à la Relish

Cooking time: 20 minutes

8 oz (225 gm) can tomato sauce
½-2 teaspoons chilli powder (this is very hot)
1 onion, finely chopped
2 tablespoons sweet pickle or chutney
1 tablespoon vinegar
1 teaspoon Worcestershire sauce
shake of pepper
pinch of salt

Put all the ingredients into a pan. Do not cover. Cook over a low heat for about 20 minutes, stirring frequently.
Makes scant ½ pint (¼ litre).

SHARP SAUCES

These sauces contrast well with bland and vegetable sauces.

Green Goddess Sauce

No cooking

6 oz (170 gm) cream cheese, softened
2 tablespoons milk
1½ tablespoons finely chopped chives
1 tablespoon chopped parsley
1 teaspoon finely chopped onion
2 teaspoons anchovy paste or ½ teaspoon anchovy essence

Blend softened cream cheese and milk. Add the rest of the ingredients, and mix well.
Makes scant ½ pint (¼ litre).

Peanut Sauce

No cooking

Blend 2 oz (55 gm) peanut butter (crunchy peanut butter is nicest); 2 teaspoons Soy sauce; 1½ teaspoons water; ¼ teaspoon sugar; ½ clove garlic, crushed, and 1 drop Tabasco sauce. Slowly stir in 3 tablespoons water.
Makes scant ¼ pint (140 ml).

Lemon Sauce

No cooking

½ pint (¼ litre) soured cream
5 tablespoons mayonnaise
1 large lemon
little chopped watercress

Blend together the soured cream, mayonnaise, the very finely grated 'zest' (yellow part) from the lemon rind, and the lemon juice. Add the finely chopped watercress.
Makes ¾ pint (425 ml).

Cheese-Gherkin Sauce

No cooking

8 oz (225 gm) cream cheese
4 tablespoons thin cream
1 teaspoon made French mustard
shake of pepper
good pinch salt
3-4 tablespoons chopped gherkins

Mix all the ingredients together.
Makes ½ pint (¼ litre).

Olive Sauce

No cooking

6 tablespoons soured cream
3 oz (85 gm) cream cheese, softened
2 tablespoons chopped olives (black, green or stuffed)
1 tablespoon finely chopped onion
1 teaspoon chopped parsley

Blend all the ingredients together.
Makes scant ½ pint (¼ litre).
NB: If soured cream is not available use natural yoghurt or thin cream and lemon juice to flavour.

Sweet-Sour Sauce

Cooking time: 10 minutes

7 tablespoons water
6 tablespoons white vinegar
8 oz (225 gm) sugar
1 small green pepper, chopped
1 small red pepper, fresh or canned, chopped
½ teaspoon salt
1 teaspoon paprika
2 teaspoons cornflour

Put 6 tablespoons each water and vinegar into a saucepan. Add the sugar and stir over a low heat until dissolved; simmer for 5 minutes. Add the chopped peppers, salt, paprika, and the cornflour, blended with the remaining water. Stir until the sauce thickens. Serve hot or cold. Makes scant ¾ pint (425 ml).

Wine Sauce

Cooking time: 12 minutes

½ pint (generous ¼ litre) Sauternes or other white wine
3 tablespoons tomato ketchup
3 level teaspoons cornflour
2 tablespoons water
½ oz (15 gm) butter or margarine

Put the wine and ketchup into a saucepan. Bring to the boil. Reduce heat; simmer for 5 minutes until slightly reduced in quantity. Blend the cornflour with the cold water; stir into wine mixture. Cook until thickened, stirring all the time. Add butter or margarine. Cook 1 minute more until the butter is absorbed.
Makes a generous ⅓ pint (185 ml).

Red Wine Sauce

Cooking time: 10 minutes

Use the recipe above but with red wine instead of white wine.

Anchovy Parsley Butter

No cooking

Beat 8 oz (225 gm) softened butter until creamy. Chop 1 oz (30 gm) canned anchovy fillets and enough parsley to give 1 tablespoon. Blend the anchovies and parsley with the butter. Allow to mellow at room temperature for at least 1 hour before serving.
Serves 10-12, and keeps well in the refrigerator.

Anchovy Butter: As above but omit parsley or use anchovy essence to taste instead of anchovy fillets.

Garlic Butter: As above but flavour with 1-2 cloves of garlic, crushed; omit anchovies and parsley.

Herb Butter: As above but flavour with up to 1 tablespoon lemon juice, and 1-2 tablespoons chopped fresh herbs (parsley, chives, thyme, basil, etc) or 1 teaspoon crushed dried herbs.

Dipping into the Cheese Pot

Cheese fondue is an ingenious Swiss concoction. This elegant dish has many uses. It can introduce a meal of meat, fish, or poultry, or stand as a main dish itself with an assortment of 'dippers' followed by a salad and dessert.

Cheese fondue is prepared just before serving. The cheese mixture may be heated in a pan over a low heat on the cooker, then transferred to the fondue pot over the fondue heater, or you may put the ingredients straight into the fondue pot and melt over the heater. The second method takes longer but has two advantages:

a   no cheese mixture is wasted, and
b   there is less possibility of the mixture becoming too hot and curdling.

A wide ceramic fondue pot enables you to stir or swirl the mixture better than when using a metal pan.

The technique of cheese fondue is simple:

1   Grate or shred the cheese so that it melts easily.
2   Make certain the cheese mixture *never* boils.
3   Add a little cornflour to minimize the possibility of curdling.
4   Keep the cheese mixture hot over the heater: *if it boils* or becomes over-heated it curdles or is 'stringy'. *If it becomes too cool* it will be tough.
5   Each person spears a 'dipper' on to the fondue fork and swirls it round in the hot cheese. There is no need to transfer the food to a dinner fork (as when cooking in oil). Wait a few seconds, then eat the delicious mixture.

A pleasant tradition is that whoever drops a bread cube into the fondue must choose and then kiss one of the guests.

For suggestions on interesting 'dippers', see page 32.

Classic Cheese Fondue

Cooking time: 10-15 minutes

> 12 oz (340 gm) Emmenthal cheese
> 4 oz (115 gm) Gruyère cheese
> 1 clove of garlic (optional)
> $\frac{1}{2}$ pint ($\frac{1}{4}$ litre) white wine—dry Sauternes or Graves
> 1 tablespoon lemon juice (optional)
> 1 teaspoon cornflour
> pinch of ground nutmeg (optional)
> shake of pepper

Make up 1 lb ($\frac{1}{2}$ kilo) cheese—the two cheeses may be used in slightly different proportions if desired.

Shred or grate the cheeses. Rub the inside of a heavy saucepan with the cut garlic clove if desired; discard garlic. Pour in nearly all the wine and lemon juice (if using this), and warm on the cooker until the surface is covered with bubbles. (Do not cover the pan or allow the mixture to boil.) Blend the cornflour with the rest of the wine, and stir into the mixture.

Remember to stir vigorously and constantly from now on. Add a little cheese, keeping the heat low, *but do not boil.* When melted, toss in more cheese. After cheese is blended and while still stirring, add ground nutmeg (if using this) and shake of pepper.

Quickly transfer the mixture to the fondue pot; keep warm over the heater. (If fondue becomes too thick, add a little warmed wine.) Spear bread cubes with fondue forks, piercing the crust last. Dip bread or other dipper into fondue and swirl to coat. The swirling is important to keep the fondue in motion.
Serves 4-6.

Suggested dippers: French bread, crusty rolls, small boiled new potatoes, raw apple and pear. *NB:* The fondue may be cooked completely over the fondue heater (see page 8).

You may omit lemon juice, and add 1-2 tablespoons brandy or Kirsch.

A crunchy morsel of French bread is swirled in the Classic Cheese Fondue. Glasses of chilled white wine make an excellent accompaniment for this sophisticated cheese and wine dish.

CLASSIC CHEESE FONDUE VARIATIONS

Traditionally, cheese fondue recipes use a well-aged natural Swiss Emmenthal cheese or a blend of Swiss Emmenthal and Gruyère. Nevertheless processed forms of these cheeses are also suitable. To give interesting flavour variation to your cheese fondue, the other natural cheeses listed below can be substituted for the Swiss cheese in Classic Cheese Fondue (see page 31). Use the quantity of cheese given in the recipe. Adjust wine and lemon juice levels as indicated below, then continue preparing the cheese fondue following the Classic Cheese Fondue method.

Several cheeses tested produced mixtures that separated into two layers of wine and cheese, or were too runny in the proportions established in the Classic Cheese Fondue recipe. These include Mozzarella and Stilton.

If you use a very mild Dutch cheese add a generous amount of lemon juice and a little less wine. If you use a processed Cheddar type cheese do the same thing. If you use a Cheddar cheese with plenty of flavour a very little port wine or brandy is an interesting addition. You can use white wine or cider. Double Gloucester and Cheshire cheese may be used in the classic fondue (as Cheddar, see above); take particular care it does not curdle.

CHEESE FONDUE DIPPERS

All dippers (ie the food put into the cheese mixture) should be bite-sized. Cut bread cubes so that each has one crust if possible (this prevents the bread crumbling). To estimate how many dippers are needed, consider appetites and accompanying dishes. Generally, 1 large loaf of French bread serves 6-8. Diced cooked meat and cooked vegetable dippers (carrots, mushrooms, etc) are best served warm; raw vegetables best at room temperature.
Choose:
  French bread; crusty rolls; bread sticks; toasted white, rye or wholemeal bread; toasted crumpets.
  Cooked prawns; diced cooked chicken or ham.
  Tiny tomatoes (these may be raw or baked); cooked Jerusalem artichokes; cooked or raw carrot slices; cooked mushrooms; raw celery or green pepper pieces; fried potato chips or slices; boiled new potatoes; raw apples and pears.

Creamy Parmesan Fondue

Cooking time: 10 minutes

½ pint (generous ¼ litre) milk
1 lb (½ kilo) cream cheese, softened
pinch of salt
½ teaspoon garlic salt
2½ oz (70 gm) grated Parmesan cheese

Beat the milk gradually into the cream cheese, mixing until well blended (an electric mixer is ideal). Heat slowly in a saucepan; add salt, garlic salt, and Parmesan cheese, stirring until smooth.

Pour into the fondue pot; place over the fondue heater. Spear dippers with fondue forks; dip into fondue, swirling to coat. (If mixture becomes too thick, stir in a little milk.)
Serves 8-10.
Suggested dippers: toast, bread sticks, warm cooked turkey or chicken.

Cheese-sour Cream Fondue

Cooking time: 12-15 minutes

6 rashers bacon
1 medium onion, chopped
2 teaspoons flour
1 lb (½ kilo) processed cheese, shredded
generous ¾ pint (425 ml) soured cream
1 teaspoon Worcestershire sauce

Chop the bacon and fry in a saucepan until crisp. Lift out of the pan, drain, and reserve 1 tablespoon bacon fat. Crumble the bacon finely; set aside. Cook the onion in the reserved fat until tender, but not brown. Stir in the flour. Add remaining ingredients. Cook *over a low heat*, stirring constantly, until the cheese has melted.

Pour into the fondue pot. Top with bacon. Place over the fondue heater. Spear dippers with fondue forks; dip into fondue.
Serves 6-8.
Suggested dippers: crispy rolls, rye bread, warm mushrooms.

Fondue Rarebit-style

Cooking time: 10 minutes

½ pint (¼ litre) white wine—dry
  Sauternes or Graves
1½ tablespoons chopped chives
½ oz (15 gm) flour
6 tablespoons water
1 lb (½ kilo) processed or Cheddar
  cheese, shredded or grated
4 egg yolks
¼ teaspoon ground nutmeg

Heat the wine and chives in a saucepan on the cooker. Blend the flour with the water. Add to the hot wine, bring to the boil, and allow to thicken slightly. Lower the heat, add the cheese, and stir constantly until cheese melts and mixture is thickened and smooth. Beat the egg yolks in a basin, whisk in 3-4 tablespoons of the hot cheese mixture. Return to the saucepan; cook and stir over a very low heat for 2-3 minutes only. Add the nutmeg. Pour into the fondue pot; place over the fondue heater. Spear pieces of French bread or mushrooms with fondue forks; dip into the cheese fondue, swirling to coat.
Serves 6-8.

Cottage Swiss Fondue

Cooking time: 10 minutes

1 oz (30 gm) butter or margarine
½ oz (15 gm) flour
pinch of garlic powder
1 teaspoon prepared mustard
½ pint (¼ litre) milk
8 oz (225 gm) cottage cheese
8 oz (225 gm) Gruyère cheese, grated
  or shredded

Melt the butter or margarine, blend in the flour, garlic powder, and mustard. Add the milk. Bring to the boil, stirring until thickened. Add the cottage and Gruyère cheeses. Beat until smooth with a whisk or emulsify in a warmed liquidizer.
  Pour into the fondue pot; place over the fondue heater. Spear 'dippers' with fondue forks, then dip into fondue, swirling to coat. (If mixture thickens upon standing, add a little milk.)
Serves 4-6.

Beer Cheese Fondue

Cooking time: 10-12 minutes

1 small clove of garlic, halved
1 tablespoon flour
10 tablespoons light beer or lager
8 oz (225 gm) Swiss processed cheese,
  shredded
4 oz (115 gm) strong Cheddar cheese,
  grated or shredded
few drops Tabasco sauce

Rub the inside of a heavy saucepan with the cut surface of garlic; discard the garlic. Blend the flour and beer or lager, pour into the pan, and stir constantly until the mixture has thickened. Add the cheeses very gradually and do not allow the mixture to become too hot. Stir in the Tabasco sauce.
  Transfer to the fondue pot; place over the heater. Spear dipper with fondue fork; dip into fondue, swirling to coat. (If the mixture becomes too thick, stir in a little additional warmed beer or lager.)
Serves 4-6.
Suggested dippers: French bread, warm boiled potatoes.
Cheddar Cider Fondue: Use cider in place of beer, and use 12 oz (340 gm) Cheddar cheese only.

Crab Cheese Fondue

Cooking time: 5-8 minutes

8 oz (225 gm) processed cheese,
  shredded
8 oz (225 gm) natural Cheddar cheese,
  grated
¼ pint (140 ml) milk
2 teaspoons lemon juice
7½ oz (215 gm) can crab meat

Stir the cheeses and milk in a pan over a low heat until melted. Add the lemon juice, stirring very well at this point, then the well drained flaked crab meat. Transfer to the fondue pot; place over the heater. Spear the dipper with fondue fork; dip in fondue, swirling to coat.
Serves 8-10.

Suggested dippers: French bread, tiny tomatoes, small cooked Jerusalem artichokes, cooked new potatoes.

From Abroad

CHINESE MENU

Chinese Hot Pot
Boiled Rice
Ginger Soy
Peanut Sauce   Red Sauce
Ice-cream   Lychees
China Tea

MEXICAN MENU

Mexi-Meatball Fondue
Creamy Avocado Sauce
Mexican Hot Sauce
Chilli-Cheese Sauce
Green Salad
Rolls   Butter   Cheese
Mexican Chocolate

Chinese Hot Pot

Cooking time: 4-6 minutes

about 12 large prawns
2 medium chicken breasts
$\frac{1}{2}$ lb (225 gm) sirloin of beef, very thinly sliced across grain
1 heart of a firm round lettuce
1 large aubergine and/or 5 oz (125 gm) can water chestnuts
4 oz (115 gm) mushrooms
8 oz (225 gm) spinach leaves
2 pints (about $1\frac{1}{4}$ litres) chicken stock, canned consommé, or water and chicken bouillon cubes
1 teaspoon grated root ginger or $\frac{1}{4}$ teaspoon ground ginger

Peel the prawns; skin, bone, and dice the chicken, and cut the meat into neat pieces. Chop the washed and dried lettuce into thick slices, dice the unpeeled aubergine and the drained water chestnuts. Wash, dry, and halve the mushrooms. Remove the stalks from the spinach and shred the leaves coarsely.

When ready to serve, put the uncooked meats and vegetables on a large tray, and the spinach in a serving bowl at room temperature. Provide chopsticks, wooden skewers, or fondue forks as cooking tools.

In a fondue cooker, frying pan or similar, heat the chicken stock, canned consommé, or water and cubes, and the ginger to simmering point. Pick up the desired food, drop into bubbling stock. When cooked, lift out and dip in selected sauce (see menu).
Serves 6.

Mexi-Meatball Fondue

Cooking time: 1-2 minutes

Combine $1\frac{1}{2}$ oz (45 gm) soft breadcrumbs (about 1 slice); up to 1 tablespoon chilli sauce (this is very hot); 1 beaten egg; $\frac{1}{4}$ teaspoon salt; 1 teaspoon chopped or dehydrated onion, and a pinch of garlic powder. Add $\frac{3}{4}$ lb (340 gm) minced beef, and mix thoroughly. Shape the mixture into about 30 meatballs.

Pour oil into the fondue pan to no more than half capacity or to a depth of 2 in (5 cm). Heat on cooker to 375°F (190°C). Transfer the pan to the fondue heater. Have the meatballs at room temperature in a serving bowl. Spear the meatballs with fondue forks, fry in hot oil for 1-2 minutes. Dip in desired sauce (see menu). Serves 3-4.

Mexican Chocolate

Cooking time: a few minutes

$1\frac{1}{2}$ pints (nearly 1 litre) milk
5 oz (140 gm) plain chocolate
6 in (15 cm) stick cinnamon
1 teaspoon vanilla essence

Combine the milk, chocolate and cinnamon stick in a saucepan. Cook over a low heat, stirring constantly, until the chocolate *just melts*. Remove the pan from the heat and take out the cinnamon stick. Stir in the vanilla, and whisk the mixture until frothy. Serve in warmed mugs, if desired.
Makes generous $1\frac{1}{2}$ pints (855 ml).

Use this type of cooker for Oriental dinners, but if you do not have one, a fondue pan or frying pan can be used instead.

WINE GUIDE

The choice of wine and other drinks served before or with food is very much a matter of personal taste, so the recommendations given are *suggestions* only for the *kind* of drinks that blend well with a particular type of food. The reason for advising a white or rosé wine to serve with fish, or delicately flavoured poultry or meat dishes is because these wines do not overpower the flavour of the food.

Game and red meat make a white or rosé wine seem a little insipid, and a full bodied red wine is the more usual and popular choice. White wines and rosé wines are served chilled, for this brings out the flavour, but *do not* over-chill. On the other hand, red wines need an hour at room temperature, with the cork drawn, to produce them at their best. The suggestions below are for easily obtainable wines.

Group	Foods Served with Group	Wine Types to Serve
APPETIZER WINES Many sherries are served at room temperature, but the drier the sherry the cooler it can be, in fact a Tio Pepe, which is one of the driest and most appreciated by connoisseurs of sherry, can be iced. Vermouth can be served with or without ice. Wines are served as recommended below.	These are the wines served before and/or with the first course.	Sherries, a dry variety is considered the best choice, but many people find this unappetizing and would prefer a medium dry sherry. Vermouth, sweet and dry. A white wine or a sparkling wine, expecially if you intend to serve this throughout the meal.
RED WINES Serve at room temperature, 60-70°F. Draw cork 1 hour before serving.	All red meats including steaks, veal; game, goose, duck, turkey; cheese (particularly strong flavoured).	Red Burgundy: Beaune, Mâcon, Beaujolais, Nuits-Saint-Georges, Volnay. Red Bordeaux: Médoc, Saint-Emilion, Pomerol, Margaux, Château Latour. Italian: Valpolicella, Tuscan Red, Chianti.
WHITE WINES Serve chilled, 45-50°F.	All poultry, chicken, turkey; fish, shell fish; veal; cheese dishes.	White Burgundy: Puligny-Montrachet. Pouilly-Fuissé, Pouilly-Fumé, Chablis, Meursault. White Bordeaux: Graves, Sauternes (drier variety). Hock: Liebfraumilch, Niersteiner. Italian: Soave, Tiroler-Riesling.
	The traditional Swiss wines served with cheese fondue.	Neuchâtel, Dézaley, Fendant de Sion.

Group	Foods Served with Group	Wine Types to Serve
ROSÉ WINES Served chilled, 45-50°F.	As an alternative to red *or* white wines (particularly good in hot weather).	Portuguese: Mateus Rosé, Justina Rosé. French: Tavel, Beaujolais Rosé.
DESSERT WINES Serve at room temperature, 60-70°F.	Alone or as after-dinner wine or with fruit, nuts, cakes, some dessert cheeses.	Port, Ruby or Tawny. Muscatel. White Tokay. Sherry, Sweet or Cream. Sweet Madeira. Sauternes, sweeter varieties.
SPARKLING WINES etc Serve chilled, 40-45°F. These wines can be kept on ice during serving.	Most types of foods.	Champagne—very dry (brut), semi-dry (sec), less dry (demi-sec), or sweet (doux). Sparkling Burgundy. Sparkling Rosé.

BEERS, LAGERS, CIDER are all good accompaniments to food.

WINES IN CHEESE FONDUE

Cheese fondue recipes using wine as an ingredient usually specify a dry white wine (the most traditional being the Swiss wine, Neuchâtel). As this wine is not readily available, choose other dry white wines.

It is possible to change the flavour of the Classic Cheese Fondue (see page 31) by using different wines; examples are given below.

If you use this wine	It gives these characteristics to the Fondue
Sherry a dry type	Either use all sherry or a mixture of sherry and white wine, this gives a more nutty flavour to the Fondue.
Champagne use a non-vintage, dry type	This gives a faintly fruity flavour to the Fondue.
Neuchâtel dry	This gives a more full bodied flavour to the Fondue.
Rhine dry	This gives a sharpness to the Fondue.
Moselle dry	The Fondue is rather delicate in flavour.
Chablis dry	The Fondue will be pale in colour and have a dry and slightly fruity flavour.
Sauternes dry	This makes the Fondue more golden in colour and it gives it a full bodied taste with a very appetizing smell.

Dessert Fondues

These are some of the least known fondues, but they will doubtless become among the most popular. Imagine dipping pieces of fresh fruit or cake, into a rich Chocolate Fondue or a refreshing Raspberry Fondue.

The 'rules' for preparing the fondue are the same as for savoury dishes. Check the temperature of oil where this is used (see page 16). Do not over-heat the mixture and allow your guests to prepare their own desserts.

The picture below shows a very attractive fondue pot suitable for heating dessert fondue mixtures, but *not for heating oil.*

DESSERT FONDUE DIPPERS

All dippers should be in bite-sized pieces, and kept at room temperature for 1 hour. Allow 8-12 pieces per serving. Drain canned or defrosted frozen fruits thoroughly. Some fresh fruit (apples, bananas, peaches, pears) discolour easily so dip in lemon juice.

Fruits to choose: apples, bananas, cherries, dates, mandarin oranges, maraschino cherries, melons, oranges, peaches, pears, pineapple, seedless grapes, strawberries.
Cakes: sponge cakes (various flavours), Madeira cake, doughnuts, wafer biscuits, crisp sweet biscuits.
Sweetmeats: marshmallows, large salted nuts, large popcorn kernels.

Butterscotch Fondue

Cooking time: 10-15 minutes

4 oz (115 gm) butter or margarine
1 lb (½ kilo) brown sugar
12 level tablespoons golden syrup
1½ tablespoons water
15 oz (about 400 gm) can sweetened condensed milk
1 teaspoon vanilla essence

Melt the butter or margarine in a strong saucepan; stir in the sugar, golden syrup, and water. Bring to the boil. Stir in the condensed milk; simmer, stirring constantly until mixture reaches the thread stage, 225°F (107°C)—this means that a little mixture, when dropped into cold water, forms a fine thread. Add the vanilla essence. Pour the sauce into the fondue pot, and place over the fondue heater. Spear dippers with fondue forks; dip in the fondue. (If mixture becomes too thick, stir in a little milk.)
Serves 8.
Suggested dippers: chocolate or coffee sponge cake, vanilla wafers, sliced apples, popcorn.

Chocolate-Cream Fondue

Cooking time: 10 minutes

8 oz (225 gm) plain or cooking chocolate
6 oz (170 gm) sugar
½ pint (¼ litre) thin cream
2 oz (55 gm) butter or margarine
2 tablespoons crème de cacao or curaçao

Put the chocolate into the top of a double saucepan or a basin and melt over hot, but not boiling water. Add the sugar, cream, and butter or margarine. Cook, stirring constantly, for about 5 minutes or until thickened. Stir in liqueur. Pour into the fondue pot; place over the fondue heater. Spear dippers with fondue forks; dip in sauce.
Serves 8-10.
Suggested dippers: coffee cake, sponge cake and Madeira cake, sliced apples, pears, maraschino cherries, marshmallows.

Toblerone Set. Spring Brothers.

Velvety Chocolate-cream Fondue provides a
sweet ending for a special meal. Pour the warm
sauce in the fondue pot just before serving; keep
warm over a low heat. Use fruit or cake dippers.

Chocolate-Nut Fondue

Cooking time: 5 minutes

> 6 oz (170 gm) plain or cooking
> chocolate
> 2 oz (55 gm) sugar
> 6 tablespoons milk
> 2 oz (55 gm) peanut butter
> 2 oz (55 gm) peanuts, walnuts or other
> nuts

Put the chocolate, sugar, and milk into the top of a double saucepan or basin over hot, but not boiling water. Cook, stirring constantly, until the chocolate has melted. Add the peanut butter; mix well, then add the minced, finely chopped or ground nuts. Pour into the fondue pot; place over fondue heater. Spear dippers with fondue forks; dip in the sauce.

Serves 6-8.

Suggested dippers: bananas, apples, Madeira cake, marshmallows.

Creamy Raspberry Fondue

Cooking time: 8-10 minutes

> 4 oz (115 gm) soft cream cheese
> 1¼ lb (625 gm) raspberries, fresh or
> defrosted
> 1 oz (30 gm) cornflour
> 6 tablespoons water
> 1 oz (30 gm) sugar
> 3 tablespoons brandy

Leave the cream cheese at room temperature for 1-2 hours. Crush the raspberries slightly in a saucepan. Blend together the cornflour and cold water, add to the berries. Cook, stirring until thickened. Sieve the mixture, discard seeds. Pour into the fondue pot; place over the fondue heater. Add the cream cheese, stirring until melted, then stir in the sugar and the brandy. Spear fruit or cake cube with fondue forks; dip in raspberry fondue.

Serves 6.

Suggested dippers: Madeira cake, pears, peaches.

NB: Use other berry fruit instead of raspberries.

Caramel Fondue

Cooking time: 8-10 minutes

Melt 1 lb (½ kilo) caramels with 4 tablespoons water in a basin over hot, but not boiling water. Stir well. Pour into the fondue pot, place over the fondue heater. (If too thick add a little extra water.) Spear dippers with fondue forks, dip in the fondue.

Serves 4.

Suggested dippers: sliced apples, bananas, peaches, marshmallows, biscuits.

French-toasted Fondue

Cooking time: 1-1½ minutes

Cut a thin loaf of French bread in bite-sized pieces. Mix 2 eggs and 4 tablespoons milk. Pour oil into the fondue pan to no more than half capacity or to a depth of 2 in (5 cm). Heat on cooker to 375°F (190°C). Transfer to fondue heater. Spear bread through crust, dip in egg mixture, fry until golden brown. Dip in Maple Syrup (page 84).

Serves 6-8.

Peppermint Fondue

Cooking time: 8-10 minutes

> 6 tablespoons milk
> 1 oz (30 gm) butter
> 1 lb (½ kilo) peppermint creams
> 2 or 3 drops green colouring

Heat all the ingredients in a saucepan over a low heat, stirring well as the mixture melts. Transfer to the fondue pot, and place over the fondue heater. Spear dippers with fondue forks and dip into the fondue.

Serves 6.

Suggested dippers: chocolate wafers, Madeira cake, sponge cake.

NB: A little crême de menthe can be added to the mixture when it is poured into the fondue pot.

Fried Cream Squares

In this recipe sponge fingers are sandwiched between cream

Cooking time: 8 minutes

2 oz (55 gm) cornflour
4 oz (115 gm) sugar
6 tablespoons milk
¾ pint (425 ml) thin cream
3 egg yolks, lightly beaten
few drops vanilla essence
few drops almond essence
about 8-10 finger (Savoy) biscuits

COATING:
2 eggs, beaten
6 oz (170 gm) ground almonds
1 oz (30 gm) fine dried breadcrumbs

FRYING:
olive or frying oil

Line the bottom and sides of a 9 in (23 cm) square tin with foil or waxed paper. Blend the cornflour, sugar, milk, and cream. Pour into a saucepan. Cook over a low heat, stirring constantly, until the mixture has thickened. Stir a small amount of the hot mixture into the egg yolks. Whisk this into the hot cornflour mixture; cook over a low heat, and stir for 2-3 minutes. Remove from the heat; add the vanilla and almond essences. Split the sponge fingers lengthways with a very sharp knife.

Spread half the hot cornflour mixture in the lined tin. Arrange sponge fingers evenly over this, then top with the remaining pudding mixture. Cover, cool, then chill thoroughly for several hours or overnight in the refrigerator—do not freeze.

Turn out onto greaseproof paper. Remove foil or waxed paper and cut into 1 in (2 cm) squares. Dip each square into the beaten eggs; coat thoroughly with a mixture of nuts and breadcrumbs. Chill, uncovered, for about 1 hour.

Pour oil into the fondue pan to no more than half capacity or to a depth of 2 in (5 cm). Heat on the cooker to 400°F (200°C). Transfer to the fondue heater. Spear dessert squares through cake layer with fondue forks; fry in the hot oil for a few seconds until browned.
Serves 14-16.

Cutting slits in the cake.
The cake with the space for the ice-cream.

Ice-cream and Cake Fondue

Cooking time: a few seconds

1 large block Neapolitan ice-cream
approximately 1 lb (½ kilo) oblong
   piece Madeira cake
2 eggs
6 tablespoons milk

FRYING:
olive or frying oil

Cut the ice-cream into eight 1 in (2 cm) cubes; freeze again until very hard (this stage is very important). Meanwhile, cut the Madeira cake into eight 1½ in (3 cm) cubes. To hollow out centres, use sharp knife to make a horizontal slit ¼ in (½ cm) from bottom of each cake cube to within ¼ in (½ cm) of the other sides (see sketch 1). Leaving ¼ in (½ cm) around all sides, cut a square straight down from top of the cube to the slit (see sketch 2). Carefully lift out. This leaves a piece of cake with ¼ in (½ cm) thick sides and bottom, and a hollow in the middle.

Insert an ice-cream cube in each hollow. Close the top of each ice-cream filled hollow with a small piece of cake. Freeze the filled pieces of cake until needed. Just before serving beat the eggs and milk. Pour into a small serving bowl.

Pour oil into the fondue pan to no more than half capacity or to a depth of 2 in (5 cm). Heat on the cooker to 400°F (200°C). Transfer the pan to the fondue heater. Spear the solidly frozen cake cubes with fondue forks; dip into the egg mixture, turning to coat all sides. Fry in the hot oil for a few seconds only, until golden brown.
Serves 4.

Fruit Fritters

Served with a tangy orange-lemon sauce

Cooking time: 12-15 minutes

1½ tablespoons orange juice
1 tablespoon sugar
2 firm bananas
1 medium eating apple
1 small fresh pineapple
4 oz (115 gm) maraschino cherries

BATTER:
4 oz (115 gm) plain flour
½ teaspoon baking powder
pinch of salt
¼ pint (140 ml) milk
1 egg, lightly beaten
1 oz (30 gm) butter or margarine, melted
¼ teaspoon lemon essence

SAUCE:
4 oz (115 gm) sugar
1 level tablespoon cornflour
pinch of salt
generous ¼ pint (140 ml) water
½ teaspoon grated orange rind
3 tablespoons orange juice
1 oz (30 gm) butter or margarine
¼ teaspoon grated lemon rind
1 tablespoon lemon juice

FRYING:
olive or frying oil

Combine the orange juice and sugar. Cut the peeled bananas, apple, and pineapple into bite-sized pieces. Let the fruit stand in the orange juice and sugar mixture until needed. Drain the maraschino cherries.

Sieve together flour, baking powder, and salt. Combine the milk, egg, melted butter or margarine, and lemon essence; add to the flour mixture, and beat until smooth.

Prepare the sauce by combining the sugar, cornflour, pinch of salt, and water in a small saucepan. Cook, stirring constantly, until thickened and smooth; continue cooking for 3 minutes. Remove from the heat; stir in the orange rind, orange juice, butter or margarine, lemon rind, and lemon juice. Keep warm.

Pour the oil into the fondue pan to no more than half capacity or to a depth of 2 in (5 cm). Heat on the cooker to 375°F (190°C). Transfer the pan to the fondue heater. Have well drained bananas, apple, pineapple, and maraschino cherries at room temperature in serving bowls.

Spear the fruit piece with a fondue fork; dip in the batter. Fry in the hot oil for 2-3 minutes or until golden brown. Dip into the warm sauce. Serves 6-8.

Mini Pastries au Fondue

Cooking time: 3-3½ minutes

1 lb (½ kilo) puff pastry (frozen or home-made)

FILLING:
chocolate covered or plain peppermint creams, glacé cherries, marshmallows, crystallized ginger, and pineapple

FRYING:
olive or frying oil

COATING:
4 oz (115 gm) sieved icing or granulated sugar
½ teaspoon ground cinnamon

Roll out pastry until wafer thin. Cut into 2 in (5 cm) squares. Place the filling in the centres. (Halve peppermint creams and marshmallows.) Fold the corners over the filling (see picture opposite), then roll into a ball. If the pastry has become a little firm damp the edges before you do this. Put into a cool place until 1 hour before serving, then arrange in serving dishes. Pour oil in fondue pan to no more than half capacity or a depth of 2 in (5 cm). Heat on the cooker to 375°F (190°C). Transfer to the fondue heater. Spear a pastry with a fondue fork. Fry in hot oil until golden brown. Dip in sugar mixed with cinnamon.
Makes 32 pastries.

These easy to make Mini Pastries are just puff pastry rolled round fruit or sweetmeats then fried in the hot oil.
In the background is an electric fondue pan. This can be set to keep the oil or fondue mixture at just the right temperature.

Tabletop Cookery

There is no doubt that tabletop cookery (this of course includes fondue cooking), is becoming one of the most popular informal ways of entertaining—and rightly so, for it has definite advantages :

1 there is no need to 'dish up' cooked food, keep it warm, transfer to serving dishes, and so on. The food is served from the cooking utensil on to individual plates, so reducing washing-up, and solving the problems of keeping food hot without it spoiling ;
2 the food is freshly cooked when the family or guests have arrived : they join in the cooking, so creating a party atmosphere very quickly ;
3 the food never becomes cold even if your guests are late.

On the other hand there are certain points to watch :
a you must take adequate precautions against accidents with hot cookers on the table ;
b you must choose the food carefully, so there is no unpleasant lingering smell of cooking in the dining-room (or pre-cook part of the dish, and just complete the cooking at the table) ;
c you do need special equipment.

The dishes in this book can all be cooked in the kitchen by 'normal' methods, so please do not imagine you *must* invest in all or any of the equipment immediately. Try out the dishes, decide which you prefer, then look at the equipment pictures, which represent *some* of the very wide range available.

If you prefer to do your cooking in the kitchen you can still create the informal atmosphere of tabletop cookery if you use 'cook and serve' type of pans. Put the food on plate warmers and let all your guests help themselves.

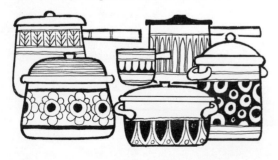

Tabletop Equipment

Fondue pans and pots have been described on pages 8 and 9, and throughout the first section of this book. Remember they can be used for cooking and heating many kinds of food.

FRYING PANS

Frying pans are some of the most suitable and versatile tabletop cooking utensils, for they enable various dishes to be cooked quickly and simply. Frying pans (particularly the electric variety) are extremely adaptable for you also can simmer, stew, and so on, very successfully in them. This is why we often use the old fashioned term 'skillet' (a metal pan with a long handle) to describe a frying pan.

SAUCEPANS AND CASSEROLES

Look around stores and shops and you will see an amazing variety of most attractive flame-proof pans and casseroles. The terms 'flame-proof' or 'heat-proof' signify that the utensil is suitable for putting on the burner, gas cooker, hotplate, electric cooker, or under a grill as well as being used in the oven or over tabletop cookers. If on the other hand a casserole is described as 'oven-proof' it means it can only be used in the oven or over a very gentle heat such as supplied by the candle-warmers, opposite.

GRILLS AND TOASTERS

Tabletop grills enable you to give an indoor barbecue ; some models are shown on page 53. The modern variations on an electric toaster provide the means of cooking complete light meals. The waffle iron, although less popular than in the USA, is another appliance that aids tabletop cookery (shown on page 85).

TABLE COOKERS

One of the easiest ways to cook at the table is to buy single or double electric, methylated spirit or picnic (bottled) gas hot-plates, then to use your gayest pots and pans on these, see opposite.

Sunbeam Electric
An electric frying pan (skillet) which is thermostatically controlled and which enables you to set the heat for all cooking processes.

Pifco
An elegant electric twin-ring cooking unit. This is thermostatically controlled, so ideal for all forms of simmering, boiling, frying, etc.

Spring Brothers
A beautiful copper flambé set (pan and spirit burners).

Jobling Housecraft Service
(Pyrex)
An oven-proof casserole, which enables you to cook the food in the oven or dish up food that has been cooked in a saucepan. This is kept warm over the heat of the 'nite-lights'.

Pifco
A small electric plate warmer (often called a hotplate). Food must be pre-cooked before being put on to this.

Spring Brothers
A stainless steel plate warmer, heated by small candles of the 'nite-light' type.
Food must be pre-cooked before being put on to this.

Appetizers and Soups

The appetizers on this and pages 48-50 are excellent for an informal party or the first course of a meal. Choose a meat based appetizer, such as the one illustrated on the opposite page, if your main course or other dishes consist of fish or cheese.

A large or electric frying pan (skillet) is excellent for serving appetizers, as they can be arranged in such a way that everyone is able to help themselves, whereas in a smaller pan they could become crushed. If you have no warming plate or heated pan, then stand the cooking container over a dish of very hot water so the food remains at a pleasantly warm temperature.

Soups may also be kept hot over containers of very hot water or on a hotplate; alternatively, you could make the soup in an electric skillet or transfer it to this when cooked. Fondue pots and pans are ideal for keeping soups at just the right heat.

TO SET AN ELECTRIC SKILLET

An electric skillet (frying pan) can be set at a given temperature and maintained at this temperature.

The information below is an approximate guide only; consult your manufacturer's instruction book.

If the skillet is set to:

200°F (90°C) the food just keeps warm.

200-250°F (90-130°C) the food simmers gently and steadily, and you can brown the outside of meat, etc *before* stewing.

250-300°F (130-150°C) steady frying; suitable for thick pieces of food (sausages), or to fry eggs.

300-350°F (150-180°C) fairly quick frying (meat or fish).

350-425°F (180-220°C) quick to immediate frying—the higher temperature is suitable only for minute steaks.

Cranberry-sauced Bites

Cooking time: 15 minutes

7½ oz (215 gm) sugar
scant ½ pint (¼ litre) water
8 oz (225 gm) fresh cranberries
3 tablespoons tomato ketchup
1 tablespoon lemon juice
1-1¼ lb (generous ½ kilo) cooked ham and chicken or turkey

Combine the sugar and water in a strong large pan, stir to dissolve the sugar. Heat to boiling; boil for 5 minutes. Add the cranberries; cook until the skins pop, about 5 minutes. Remove from the heat. Stir in the ketchup and lemon juice. Pour into smaller saucepan or flame-proof pan.* Cut the ham and chicken or turkey into neat cubes; place in the sauce. Keep warm over hot water or a low heat. Spear with cocktail sticks.
Makes generous ¾ pint (425 ml) sauce.

*NB: A fondue pan is excellent for this, or use a deep skillet (picture right) or electric skillet set to 225°F (110°C).

Duo Cheese Dip

Cooking time: 12 minutes

1 oz (30 gm) butter
1 oz (30 gm) flour
½ pint (¼ litre) beef stock
1-2 teaspoons chopped onion
½ teaspoon Tabasco sauce
3 tablespoons thick cream
4 oz (115 gm) Cheddar cheese
4 oz (115 gm) Gruyère cheese

Make a coating sauce with butter, flour and stock. Lower the heat, add the onion, Tabasco sauce, cream, and grated cheeses. Season if required. Keep warm, and serve with small biscuits and crisps.
Makes generous ¾ pint (425 ml).

Delicious Cranberry-sauced Bites add a splash of colour to the buffet table.

Crab-stuffed Mushrooms

Cooking time: 10 minutes

1 lb ($\frac{1}{2}$ kilo) fresh small mushrooms
3$\frac{1}{2}$ oz (95 gm) butter or margarine, melted
2 tablespoons fine dried breadcrumbs
1$\frac{1}{2}$ tablespoons finely chopped celery
1 tablespoon finely chopped canned or fresh red pepper
$\frac{1}{2}$ teaspoon chopped onion, fresh or dehydrated
$\frac{1}{4}$ teaspoon dry mustard
7-8 oz (200-225 gm) fresh or canned crab meat
8 tablespoons soured cream
8 tablespoons mayonnaise or salad cream
2 tablespoons milk
2 teaspoons lemon juice
1 teaspoon prepared mustard

Set electric skillet to 225°F (110°C). Remove stems from mushrooms. Place unfilled mushrooms, rounded side up, in a grill pan. Brush tops with 2 oz (55 gm) of the butter or margarine. Grill for 2-3 minutes. Remove from grill.*

Combine the breadcrumbs, the remaining 1$\frac{1}{2}$ oz (40 gm) butter or margarine, celery, red pepper, onion, and dry mustard. Stir in the crab meat. Turn mushrooms, fill each with crab mixture.

In a pan or skillet combine the soured cream, mayonnaise or salad cream, milk, lemon juice, and prepared mustard. Cook, stirring until hot, lower the heat to 200°F (90°C). Arrange filled mushrooms, rounded side down, in sauce. Heat through.
Makes 36-48 appetizers.

*NB: This could be done beforehand.

Chilli-Cheese Dip

Cooking time: 15 minutes

Tip approximately 1 lb ($\frac{1}{2}$ kilo) canned chilli with beans into a pan, mash, heat with 1 teaspoon Worcestershire sauce, 3 tablespoons beer, and 3 tablespoons thick cream. Add 8 oz (225 gm) grated Cheddar cheese.
Makes 1$\frac{1}{4}$ pints (710 ml).

Cheese-Bacon Dip

Cooking time: 12 minutes

6 rashers bacon
8 oz (225 gm) cream cheese
8 oz (225 gm) processed or Cheddar cheese, shredded or grated
6 tablespoons milk
$\frac{1}{4}$ teaspoon onion or garlic salt
$\frac{1}{4}$ teaspoon dry mustard
3-4 drops Tabasco sauce

Grill or fry the bacon until crisp, then crumble. In a small pan melt the cream cheese *slowly,* stirring constantly. Add the processed or Cheddar cheese, milk, onion or garlic salt, mustard, and Tabasco sauce. Cook, stirring constantly, until the cheese melts. Add the bacon. Keep warm over hot water or a very low heat. Serve with assorted biscuits. (If mixture becomes too thick, stir in a little milk.)
Makes a generous $\frac{1}{2}$ pint ($\frac{1}{4}$ litre).
NB: This may also be prepared in a fondue pan.

Chilli-Cheese Dip served with potato crisps.

Crab-Cheese Dip

Cooking time: 8-10 minutes

1½ tablespoons finely chopped onion
1½ tablespoons finely chopped green
   pepper
1 oz (30 gm) butter or margarine
10½ oz (295 gm) can condensed cream
   of mushroom soup
6 tablespoons milk
6 oz (170 gm) Cheddar cheese, grated
2 eggs, beaten
6-7 oz (170-200 gm) fresh or canned
   crab meat, flaked
pinch of ground nutmeg

Set electric skillet to 250°F (130°C). Cook the onion and green pepper in a pan with the butter or margarine until tender but *not brown.* Stir in the soup, then gradually blend in the milk. Cook, stirring until bubbly. Add the cheese to the soup mixture; stir until melted (reduce the heat slightly). Stir 2-3 tablespoons cheese mixture into the beaten eggs; return to the hot mixture. Cook and stir for 2 minutes. Add crab and nutmeg. Keep warm over a low heat. Serve with biscuits.
Makes scant 1½ pints (¾ litre).

Lobster Dip Elégante

Cooking time: 8-10 minutes

8 oz (225 gm) cream cheese
3 tablespoons mayonnaise or salad
   cream
1 clove garlic, crushed
1 teaspoon sugar
1 teaspoon prepared mustard
1 teaspoon grated onion
pinch of seasoned salt
5 oz (140 gm) fresh or well drained
   canned lobster
2 tablespoons Sauternes or other white
   wine

In a small pan melt the cream cheese *slowly,* stirring constantly. Blend in the mayonnaise or salad cream, garlic, sugar, mustard, onion, and seasoned salt. Stir in the lobster and wine; heat through. Keep warm over hot water or a very low heat. Serve with Melba toast and assorted biscuits.
Makes scant ¾ pint (425 ml).

Elegant Salmon Balls

Cooking time: 20 minutes

1 lb (½ kilo) canned salmon
   (pink salmon can be used)
2 oz (55 gm) soft breadcrumbs
2 eggs
2½ tablespoons chopped parsley
1 small onion, finely chopped
2 teaspoons lemon juice
salt and pepper
8 tablespoons white wine
1 oz (30 gm) butter or margarine
¾ oz (25 gm) flour
6 tablespoons thin cream
1 tablespoon capers, drained

Set electric skillet to 250°F (130°C). Drain the salmon, reserving the liquid. Remove the fish skin and bones, and flake the fish into a bowl. Add the breadcrumbs, eggs, 1½ tablespoons of the parsley, the onion, lemon juice, a pinch of salt, and a shake of pepper. Mix well and form into 16 small balls. Chill well.

Pour the wine and strained salmon liquid into a measure, add enough water to make a generous ½ pint (¼ litre). Heat the butter or margarine in a pan, stir in the flour, and cook for several minutes. Gradually blend in the wine liquid, and stir until thickened and smooth. Remove from the heat, add the cream, remaining parsley, capers, and seasoning to taste. Either leave in the pan or pour into the skillet. Place the salmon balls into the sauce, and heat gently for 10 minutes.

Makes 16 appetizers.

Creamy Seafood Dip

Cooking time: 10 minutes

Use about 8 oz (225 gm) cockles; prawns; canned clams or other shell fish. Pour 2 tablespoons milk, or the liquid from the can into a pan, blend with 8 oz (225 gm) soft cream cheese, 1 crushed clove of garlic, the fish, and a squeeze of lemon juice. Heat gently.

Makes generous ½ pint (¼ litre).

Sweet-sour Surprises

Cooking time: 15 minutes

3 oz (85 gm) butter or margarine
8 oz (225 gm) tiny meatballs (see
   page 12)
8 oz (225 gm) chicken livers
pinch of salt
8 oz (225 gm) shelled prawns
½ oz (15 gm) cornflour
1 oz (30 gm) sugar
1 chicken bouillon cube
scant ½ pint (¼ litre) pineapple juice
6 tablespoons water
4 tablespoons vinegar
1½ tablespoons Soy sauce

Set electric skillet to 225°F (110°C). Heat 2½ oz (70 gm) of the butter or margarine, and brown the meatballs and chicken livers, season lightly. Mix with the prawns and put on one side. This can be done beforehand.

Blend the cornflour, sugar and crushed bouillon cube. Add the pineapple juice, water, vinegar, Soy sauce, and remaining ½ oz (15 gm) butter. Pour into the pan or skillet, and stir over the heat until boiling. Cover with a lid, simmer for 5 minutes. Arrange meats and prawns in sauce. Heat through. Lower the heat and keep warm. Spear with cocktail sticks.

Makes 60-65 appetizers.

Hot Tomato Cocktail

Cooking time: 5 minutes

2 pints (1¼ litres) tomato juice
10½ oz (295 gm) can beef consommé or
   ¾ pint (435 ml) good beef stock
1 teaspoon grated onion
1 teaspoon grated horseradish
1 teaspoon Worcestershire sauce
1-2 drops Tabasco sauce
8 lemon slices
8 cocktail onions

Bring ingredients to the boil; keep warm. Top with lemon slices and cocktail onions.

Serves 8.

Syrup Appetizers

Tasty idea for a party

Cooking time: 12 minutes

1 lb (½ kilo) pork sausages (skinless
   if possible)
12 oz (340 gm) can pineapple chunks
1 level tablespoon cornflour
½ teaspoon salt
3-4 tablespoons maple syrup or golden
   syrup (if maple syrup is unobtainable)
4 tablespoons water
4 tablespoons vinegar
1 medium green pepper
2-3 tablespoons drained maraschino
   cherries

Set electric skillet to 250°F (130°C). Cut the sausages across in thirds, cook and brown in the skillet. Use a very little fat if necessary. (This can be done beforehand.) Remove the sausages to a dish. Drain the pineapple, reserve 8 tablespoons syrup. At serving time blend the cornflour, salt, reserved pineapple syrup, maple or golden syrup, water and vinegar in an attractive bowl. Pour into the skillet and bring to boil, stirring constantly; cook, stirring for 2-3 minutes longer. Cut the green pepper into ½ in (1 cm) squares, discard core and seeds. Add the drained pineapple, sausage pieces, green pepper chunks, and cherries; heat through. Lower heat and keep warm. Spear with cocktail sticks.

Serves 6-8.

Vegetable-Scampi Gumbo

Delicious creamy flavour

Cooking time: 10 minutes

Grate 3 large carrots and 1 onion finely. Put into a pan with 3 tablespoons water. Add seasoning, cover the pan. Cook until the vegetables are tender (about 5 minutes). Add two 10½ oz (295 gm) cans scampi soup, ¼ pint (140 ml) milk and shake of pepper. Stir as the mixture heats.

Serves 4-5.

Asparagus-Cheese soup

Cooking time: 20 minutes

small bundle fresh or 8 oz (225 gm)
  frozen asparagus
salt
½ oz (15 gm) butter or margarine
2 teaspoons flour
generous ¾ pint (425 ml) milk
2-3 drops Tabasco sauce
shake of pepper
4 oz (115 gm) Dutch Gouda cheese,
  grated

Cook the asparagus in salted water until tender; drain, then chop. This is best done beforehand, as it has a rather strong smell. Melt the butter or margarine in a pan. Blend in the flour. Add the milk gradually; cook, stirring constantly, until thickened. Add the asparagus, ¼ teaspoon salt, Tabasco sauce, and pepper; mix well. Add the cheese; heat, stirring constantly, until melted. Keep warm but do not heat again.

Serves 4-6.

Onion-Wine Soup

Cooking time: 10-12 minutes

2 oz (55 gm) butter or margarine
3 medium onions, thinly sliced
2 pints (1¼ litres) very good chicken
  stock
6 tablespoons dry white wine
8-10 small slices French bread,
  toasted if desired
grated Parmesan cheese

Heat the butter or margarine in a pan, then cook the onion until lightly browned. Add the stock, just over ½ pint (¼ litre) water, and the wine; heat. Ladle into soup bowls. Sprinkle bread or toast slices with cheese; float on soup. Serve additional cheese as an accompaniment if desired.

Serves 8-10.

NB: This soup is really better if made previously, then reheated. Naturally the bread or toast and cheese must be added at the last minute. Add 1-2 crushed cloves of garlic to the onions for a stronger flavour.

Cream of Corn Soup

Cooking time: 12 minutes

1 oz (30 gm) butter or margarine
1 large onion, finely chopped
2 medium carrots, grated
1 small green pepper
½ oz (15 gm) flour
shake of pepper
2 chicken bouillon cubes
¾ pint (425 ml) milk
14 oz (400 gm) can cream-style corn

Heat the butter or margarine in a pan, then cook the onion, carrots, and finely chopped green pepper until tender. Discard the core and seeds of the pepper. Blend in the flour, and a shake of pepper. Add the crushed bouillon cubes, milk, and corn. Cook, stirring occasionally, until the mixture bubbles.

Serves 4-6.

Onion-Cheddar Soup

Cooking time: 10-12 minutes

1½ oz (45 gm) butter or margarine
1 large onion, chopped
¾ oz (25 gm) flour
½ teaspoon salt
shake of pepper
1½ pints (¾ litre) milk
8 oz (225 gm) Cheddar cheese, grated

GARNISH:
paprika
chives, chopped

Heat the butter or margarine in a pan, then cook the onion until tender but not brown. (For a stronger flavour, add 1-2 crushed cloves of garlic to the onions.) Blend in the flour, salt, and pepper. Gradually blend in the milk. Bring to the boil, stirring constantly, and continue cooking until slightly thickened. Remove from the heat. Add the cheese, stirring until melted. Keep warm but do not cook again. Ladle into soup bowls. Garnish each serving with paprika and chopped chives.

Serves 4-6.

Fish Dishes

When choosing fish for tabletop cookery avoid recipes that need prolonged cooking, for the shorter the cooking time, the less smell of fish will be in the dining-room. Most of the recipes that follow are for shell fish, for these cook or heat quickly, taste delicious, and look attractive when prepared. Never over-cook shell fish, for it makes the texture tough and hard.

Cantonese Prawns

Cooking time: 15 minutes

> 1 tablespoon salad oil
> 4-6 oz (115-170 gm) 'mange-tout' peas (see below)
> generous ¼ pint (140 ml) chicken stock
> 5 oz (140 gm) can water chestnuts
> ¼ teaspoon salt
> 1 tablespoon cornflour
> 3 tablespoons cold water
> 5-6 oz (140-170 gm) shelled or canned prawns (or shrimps)

Mange-tout peas are the very tender French peas where pods and peas are cooked together for a few minutes. If not available use frozen peas. A very good shop may well sell Chinese peas (frozen or canned).

Set electric skillet to 250°F (130°C). Heat the oil in the skillet. Toss the peas in this for 2-3 minutes. Stir in the chicken stock, the drained and sliced chestnuts and salt. Cover and cook for 2 minutes, stirring once or twice.

Combine the cornflour and cold water; add to the mixture in the skillet. Cook, stirring constantly, until mixture is thickened and clear, about 2 minutes. Add the prawns or shrimps (drain the canned variety); toss gently to mix. Heat thoroughly.
Serves 2-3.

Barbecued Prawn Kebabs

The following sauce can be used instead to vary seafood kebabs. If time allows leave filled skewers in the sauce for 15 minutes before cooking.

For the sauce: blend 3 tablespoons salad oil, 2 tablespoons vinegar, 1 tablespoon brown sugar, and 3 tablespoons tomato ketchup.

Curried Shrimp Skillet

Cooking time: 15-20 minutes

> 1 oz (30 gm) butter or margarine
> 1 medium-sized apple, peeled and chopped
> 6 tablespoons sliced celery
> 1 level teaspoon curry powder
> generous ¾ pint (425 ml) chicken stock, or water and 1 chicken bouillon cube
> 10 oz (285 gm) can macaroni cheese *
> pinch of salt
> shake of pepper
> 5-6 oz (140-170 gm) can shrimps or prawns, drained

Set electric skillet to 250°F (130°C). Melt butter or margarine in the skillet. Add the apple, celery, and curry powder; cook until just tender, but retain the crisp texture of the celery. Reduce heat (re-set electric skillet to 200-225°F (90-110°C)); add stock or water and bouillon cube, macaroni cheese, and salt. Cover skillet. Cook over a low heat until macaroni is very hot, about 5 minutes, stirring occasionally; add seasoning to taste. Top macaroni cheese mixture with drained shrimps. Heat through.
Serves 4-6.
*NB: This is an excellent way to use up left over macaroni cheese.

Lemon-Prawn Kebabs

Inviting for appetizers or main course

Cooking time: 4-6 minutes

1-2 tablespoons chilli sauce
   (see below)
2 tablespoons salad oil
1½ tablespoons golden syrup or black
   treacle
1¼ tablespoons vinegar
½ clove garlic
½ teaspoon salt
¼ teaspoon pepper
2 lemons, cut into small wedges
1½-2 lb (¾-1 kilo) shelled large Dublin
   Bay prawns

Chilli sauce is *very* hot so add gradually. Many people will like a few drops only.

In a liquidizer goblet combine the chilli sauce, salad oil, syrup or treacle, vinegar, garlic, salt and pepper; cover and blend on high speed of liquidizer until the sauce is smooth. If you have added very little chilli sauce, taste, increase the amount if desired.

   Thread the lemon wedges and prawns on skewers. Cook over the barbecue or under the grill for 4-6 minutes, turning once, and brushing with sauce occasionally. To serve, squeeze the juice from the hot lemon wedges over the prawns.

Makes 10-12 appetizers or 6 main courses.

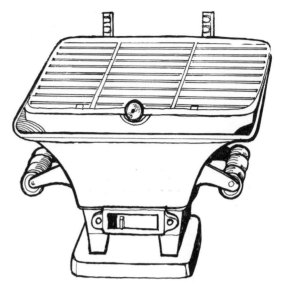

A cast-iron charcoal habachi grill (or indoor barbecue) ideal for kebabs, meat, etc. This can be used indoors, but it is better put in a fireplace, on a wide window sill or side table, near a window, or on a balcony. Allow the charcoal to heat through and become a dullish glowing red before using (this takes about 40 minutes).
There are 3 cooking heights.

USING TABLE GRILLS

Grilling has become one of the most popular forms of cooking, which is not surprising when one considers its many good points. Grilling is quick and easy, less fat is used than when frying food, so it is less fattening and more health giving. Choose really tender meat and young chicken joints for grilling; pre-heat the grill before cooking. Tabletop grills vary a great deal, so you have a splendid choice. The Oriental inspired habachi is shown on this page with a modern rotisserie type (see also pages 65 and 72).

Moulinex Rotisserie
A modern electric rotisserie. Ideal for kebabs, whole or jointed chickens, and pieces of meat. This is self-cleaning.

Seafood in Wine

Cooking time: depends upon fish plus few minutes

about 1 lb (½ kilo) assorted fresh, frozen, or canned shell fish (lobster, crab, shrimps, or scallops)
6 tablespoons dry white wine
3 tablespoons salad oil
2 teaspoons finely chopped onion
pinch of sugar
¼ teaspoon salt
pinch of dried rosemary leaves, crushed
shake of pepper
1 oz (30 gm) butter or margarine, melted
1 tablespoon lemon juice

Set electric skillet to 225°F (110°C). Cook any shell fish that is not ready prepared in salted water; cool. (Remove meat from shells, if necessary.) Cut into bite-sized pieces. Blend the wine, oil, onion, sugar, salt, rosemary, and pepper; pour over the fish. Marinate for a few hours in the refrigerator, stirring occasionally. When serving, drain the seafood, reserving the marinade. Place the seafood in a pan or skillet. Combine the marinade, butter or margarine, and lemon juice. Pour over the seafood, heat gently. Spear with cocktail sticks.

Makes 50 appetizers.

Toast Cups

Cooking time: 8-15 minutes

9 small thin slices fresh white bread
2-3 oz (55-85 gm) butter, softened

Trim the crusts from the bread, then roll the bread with a rolling pin to make it more 'pliable'. Press into ungreased patty tins and spread or brush with the softened butter. Bake just above the centre of a very moderate oven, 325-350°F (170-180°C), Gas No 3-4, for 15 minutes or until crisp. If you wish to shorten the cooking time allow 8-10 minutes in a moderately hot oven. This does not give such even browning.

Makes 9 cups.

Lobster Newberg

Cooking time: 15-20 minutes

3 oz (85 gm) butter or margarine
½ oz (15 gm) flour
generous ½ pint (285 ml) thin cream
3 egg yolks, beaten
small fresh lobster or 6 oz (170 gm) canned lobster
2 tablespoons dry white wine
2 teaspoons lemon juice
pinch of salt
paprika
Toast Cups

Melt the butter or margarine in a pan; blend in the flour. Add the cream gradually. Cook over a low heat, stirring constantly, until thickened. Pour into a fondue pot or into a basin over hot water or the top of a double pan. Stir a small amount of the hot mixture into the beaten egg yolks; then return to the hot mixture. Heat, stirring constantly, until the mixture thickens again. Flake the lobster, add to the sauce and heat through. Stir in the wine, lemon juice, and salt. Sprinkle with paprika. Serve in Toast Cups.

Serves 4-6.

Speedy Prawn Newberg

Cooking time: 10 minutes

2 15 oz (425 gm) cans cream of scampi soup
¼ pint (140 ml) milk or thin cream
2 tablespoons dry sherry
4-6 oz (100-150 gm) cooked or canned peas
24 large shelled prawns (approximately)
4 oz (115 gm) Cheddar cheese, grated

Heat the soup with the milk or thin cream and sherry, add the peas, prawns, and cheese, and heat again. In the picture opposite, the Prawn Newberg is kept warm over a container of hot water, but an electric plate warmer or fondue heater would be ideal.

Serve with crisp toast or crisp puff pastry cases, as illustrated opposite.

Serves 4-6.

Dish for a special occasion – Speedy Prawn Newberg.

Prawn Curry

Cooking time: 15 minutes

2 oz (55 gm) butter or margarine
1 medium-sized onion, chopped
2 sticks celery, chopped
1 small apple, peeled and chopped
1-2 teaspoons curry powder
10½ oz (295 gm) can condensed cream
    of celery soup
sliced mushrooms (optional)
½ lb (225 gm) prawns, halved lengthwise

TO SERVE:
cooked rice

Set the electric skillet to *just* 340°F (175°C). Heat the butter or margarine, and cook the onion, celery, apple, and curry powder for a few minutes. Stir in the soup and a few sliced mushrooms. Simmer, uncovered, for 5 minutes, then add the prawns and cook for a further 3-4 minutes; stirring often. Serve over rice. Serves 4.

Tuna Pilaff

Cooking time: 10-12 minutes

2-4 oz (55-115 gm) mushrooms
2 medium-sized onions
2 oz (55 gm) butter or margarine
3 tablespoons finely chopped celery
1 small green pepper, finely chopped
8 oz (225 gm) cooked rice *
7 oz (200 gm) can tuna, drained
1 teaspoon Worcestershire sauce
½ teaspoon salt
pinch of dried thyme
shake of pepper

*about 3 oz (85 gm) before cooking

Set electric skillet to 300°F (150°C). Cut the mushrooms and onion into neat slices and toss in the hot butter or margarine for a few minutes. Add the celery, green pepper, rice, tuna, Worcestershire sauce, salt, thyme, and pepper; toss to mix. Reduce heat to 200°F (90°C); cook, stirring until heated through. If the mixture seems a little dry add a few tablespoons water or chicken stock. Serves 4.

Potato-Fish Fillets

Cooking time: 10 minutes

2 lb (1 kilo) fillets of fresh haddock,
    cod or whiting
½ teaspoon garlic salt
6 tablespoons powdered instant
    mashed potatoes
2 tablespoons salad oil
¾ pint (425 ml) chicken stock, or water
    and ½ chicken bouillon cube
2 tablespoons powdered instant
    mashed potatoes
1½ tablespoons finely chopped onion
1 tablespoon lemon juice
2-3 teaspoons chopped parsley

Set electric skillet to 375°F (190°C). Cut the fish into serving-sized pieces. Sprinkle both sides with garlic salt. Roll the pieces of fish in the 6 tablespoons powdered instant mashed potatoes. Heat the oil and fry the fish in the hot oil until browned, turning once. Remove from the skillet to a warm serving dish. Blend the remaining ingredients in the skillet; simmer, stirring constantly, until thickened; lower the heat when the mixture starts to simmer. Serve the hot savoury potato sauce with the fish. Serves 6-8.

The picture above shows Sweet-sour Surprises, recipe on page 50. Although this can be served as an appetizer it is sufficiently substantial for a main dish too.

Fish Meunière

Cooking time: from 10 minutes

4 large fillets or cutlets of white fish, sole, plaice, etc
seasoning
3 oz (85 gm) butter
juice of 1 lemon
1-2 tablespoons chopped parsley
1-2 teaspoons capers (optional)

Set electric skillet to 300°F (150°C). Wash and dry the fish, season well. Heat the butter in the frying pan and cook the fish until tender. Lift onto hot serving plates or a dish, allow the butter to become golden brown, add the lemon juice, parsley, and capers, heat thoroughly, then spoon over the fish.
Serves 4.

Sweet-sour Prawns

Cooking time: 15 minutes

1½ oz (45 gm) sugar
½ oz (15 gm) cornflour
scant ½ pint (¼ litre) chicken stock, or water and ½ chicken bouillon cube
¼ pint (140 ml) canned pineapple juice
3 tablespoons vinegar
1-1½ tablespoons Soy sauce
½ oz (15 gm) butter or margarine
6 oz (170 gm) can bean shoots, drained
6 oz (170 gm) canned, drained, or peeled prawns

TO SERVE:
cooked rice

Set electric skillet to 225-250°F (110-130°C). Blend the sugar and cornflour with the chicken stock or water and bouillon cube. Add the pineapple juice, vinegar, Soy sauce, and butter or margarine. Cook, stirring constantly, until the mixture thickens. Cover and simmer 5 minutes longer. Stir in the bean shoots and prawns; heat through. Serve prawn mixture over hot cooked rice.
Serves 4-5

Sunbeam Automatic Frypan
The picture above shows the first stage of Fish Meunière, the fish being cooked in the hot butter.

Pyrosil Pan
The frying pan above, which also can be used as a shallow saucepan or casserole (it has a glass lid), can be used on top of an ordinary cooker then brought to the table and kept hot over a fondue heater or plate warmer.

Meat Dishes

There is an excellent choice of meat dishes for tabletop cookery. Most stews can be kept warm or even cooked at the table; fried and grilled meats of all kinds are also suitable.

Slow cooking stews can be partially cooked in the kitchen, then brought into the dining-room to complete the cooking process.

The Deutsch Dinner opposite provides a complete main course in just one dish.

Deutsch Dinner

Cooking time: 20 minutes

5 rashers bacon
2 medium-sized onions, chopped
scant $\frac{1}{2}$ pint ($\frac{1}{4}$ litre) mayonnaise or
   salad cream
$\frac{1}{2}$ teaspoon salt
dash of pepper
1 teaspoon celery seeds
6 tablespoons water
$1\frac{1}{2}$-2 tablespoons vinegar
1-$1\frac{1}{4}$ lb (generous $\frac{1}{2}$ kilo) cooked
   potatoes
$\frac{1}{2}$ lb ($\frac{1}{4}$ kilo) knackwurst, cut in $\frac{1}{2}$ in
   (1 cm) slices and skinned
4 tablespoons sweet pickle
1 tablespoon chopped canned red
   pepper (pimento)

GARNISH:
1 hard-boiled egg, sliced
parsley (optional)

Set electric skillet to 275°F (140°C). Fry or grill the bacon until crisp; drain and crumble, reserving the bacon fat. Heat this fat in a large flame-proof pan or electric skillet, and cook the onions until tender. Blend in the mayonnaise or salad cream, salt, pepper, and celery seeds. Add the water and vinegar; heat gently. Cut the potatoes into neat cubes and add this, the knackwurst, bacon, pickle, and pimento to the sauce. Heat through, tossing lightly, lower heat to keep warm. Garnish with egg and parsley, if desired.

Serves 5-6.

Deutsch Dinner – a nourishing meal attractively served.

Burgundied Fillet Steak

Cooking time: 15 minutes

1½ lb (¾ kilo) fillet steak, cut into
  thin slices
salt
3 oz (85 gm) butter
2 medium-sized green peppers
2 medium-sized onions, chopped
nearly ½ pint (¼ litre) beef stock or
  canned beef consommé
6 tablespoons red Burgundy
1½ tablespoons cornflour
pepper

Set electric skillet to 375°F (190°C). Cut the meat into strips about 2-3 in (5-8 cm) in length. Sprinkle the meat with ½ teaspoon salt. Melt 1 oz (30 gm) of the butter in skillet. Brown a third of the meat in the butter; remove to a warmed serving dish. Repeat twice with remaining meat adding butter as needed. Lower heat or re-set electric skillet to 275°F (140°C). Dice the green peppers, discard the cores and seeds.

Add any remaining butter, the diced green peppers, and onions to the pan, cook for about 3 minutes. Add stock or consommé. Blend the wine and cornflour; stir into the liquid. Cook, stirring constantly, until thickened. Cook and stir for a further 2 minutes. Season with salt and pepper. Add the meat, and heat through.
Serves 6.
NB: Serve with creamed potatoes, with boiled rice or noodles.

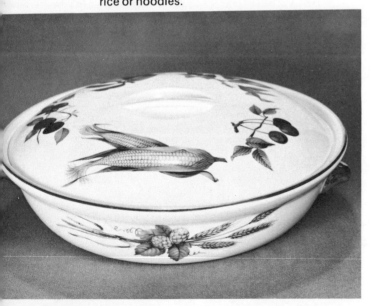

Classic Beef Stroganoff

Cooking time: 15-18 minutes

3 oz (85 gm) butter
3 oz (85 gm) mushrooms, sliced
3 level tablespoons flour
½ teaspoon salt
1 lb (½ kilo) sirloin or fillet steak,
  cut in ¼ in (½ cm) strips
2 medium-sized onions, finely chopped
1 clove garlic, finely chopped
½ pint (¼ litre) beef stock or canned
  beef consommé
1 tablespoon tomato paste
scant ½ pint (¼ litre) soured cream
1½ tablespoons dry sherry

Set electric skillet to 375°F (190°C). Heat 1 oz (30 gm) of the butter in the skillet, and fry the sliced mushrooms for a few minutes. Combine 1 tablespoon of flour and the salt; coat the meat with the flour mixture. Melt another 1 oz (30 gm) butter in the skillet, put in the meat, and brown quickly on both sides; remove from pan, then add the onions and garlic and cook for 3-4 minutes until the onion is soft. Remove onions, mix with the meat and mushrooms. (This can be done beforehand, but do not over-cook the meat.) Lower the heat or re-set electric skillet to 275°F (140°C).

Add the remaining butter to the pan drippings; blend in the remaining flour. Stir in the stock or consommé. Bring to the boil and stir well until thickened; add the tomato paste. Return the meat mixture to the skillet. Heat for a few minutes, stir in the soured cream and sherry; cook slowly until heated (*do not boil*). Serve at once.
Serves 4.
NB: Serve with boiled noodles or rice or new potatoes.

TO VARY:
Use the recipe above, but substitute beer for beef stock. Omit the tomato paste and add a few drops of Worcestershire sauce and ¼ teaspoon paprika to the mixture.

An elegant and practical flame-proof casserole (left).

Beef and Fruit Kebabs

Cooking time: 6-8 minutes

- ¾ lb (340 gm) fillet or rump steak, cut in 1 in (2 cm) slices
- 11 oz (310 gm) can mandarin oranges
- 13½ oz (385 gm) can pineapple chunks
- 2 oz (55 gm) brown sugar
- 2-3 tablespoons honey
- ½ oz (15 gm) butter or margarine, melted

Cut the meat into 1 in (2 cm) squares. Drain the oranges and pineapple, reserving 4 tablespoons syrup. Alternate meat and fruit on four long skewers. (Skewer oranges crosswise.) Blend the reserved syrup and remaining ingredients. Cook kebabs over the barbecue or under the grill for about 6-8 minutes; turn to brown on all sides and baste frequently with the sauce.

Serves 4.

Teriyaki Appetizers

Cooking time: 5-6 minutes

- 1½ lb (¾ kilo) sirloin steak, cut in about 1 in (2 cm) slices
- 5 oz (140 gm) canned water chestnuts

MARINADE:
- 6 tablespoons Soy sauce
- 2 oz (55 gm) brown sugar
- 1½ tablespoons salad oil
- 1 tablespoon grated fresh ginger root or 1 teaspoon ground ginger
- ¼ teaspoon freshly ground pepper
- 2 cloves garlic, finely chopped

Cut the meat into very thin strips. Drain and halve the water chestnuts. In a deep bowl combine all the ingredients; toss gently to coat the meat and chestnuts. Leave for 2 hours at room temperature. Drain the meat and chestnuts, reserving the marinade.

Thread the meat strips on metal skewers accordian-style; then add a water chestnut. Grill for 5-6 minutes, turning frequently. Baste with the marinade.

Serves 6-8.

Devilled Steak

Cooking time: 10 minutes

Set electric skillet to 300°F (150°C). Grill 1½ lb (¾ kilo) sirloin steak very lightly, basting with 1-2 oz (30-55 gm) melted butter. Melt 1 oz (30 gm) butter in the skillet, add 1 tablespoon chopped parsley, 2 tablespoons sherry, 1 teaspoon dry mustard, 1 teaspoon Worcestershire sauce, ¼ teaspoon salt, and a shake of pepper. Add the steak. Pour 2 tablespoons brandy over the meat, etc, and ignite. When flames die, remove steak, and cut into 6 pieces; keep hot. Stir 2 oz (55 gm) sliced mushrooms, and 3 tablespoons tomato ketchup or fresh tomato purée into the pan. Simmer for 5 minutes. Serve over the steak.

Serves 6, or makes 12 appetizers.

Sweet-sour Burgers

Cooking time: 25 minutes

- 8-9 oz (225-255 gm) can tomato sauce
- 6 gingernut biscuits, crushed
- 4 tablespoons finely chopped onion
- 1½ oz (45 gm) raisins
- 1 egg, beaten
- ¼ teaspoon salt
- 1½ lb (¾ kilo) raw minced beef
- ½ tablespoon oil
- 1 oz (30 gm) brown sugar
- 1 tablespoon vinegar
- 1 teaspoon prepared mustard
- shake of pepper

Set electric skillet to 225-250°F (110-130°C). Combine 3 tablespoons of the tomato sauce, the gingernuts, onion, raisins, egg, and salt. Add the meat; mix well. Shape into 6 round flat patties. Heat the small quantity of oil, then brown the meat patties on both sides. Combine the remaining tomato sauce, the brown sugar, vinegar, mustard, and pepper; pour over the burgers. Cover the pan and simmer for 20 minutes, spooning sauce over the burgers occasionally. Lower the heat if necessary.

Serves 6.

Beef and Cauliflower Sweet and Sour

Cooking time: 12-15 minutes

1 small cauliflower
salt
8 oz (225 gm) green beans, fresh or
  frozen
1 lb ($\frac{1}{2}$ kilo) sirloin steak
2 tablespoons dry sherry
shake of pepper
1$\frac{1}{2}$ tablespoons salad oil
$\frac{1}{2}$ oz (15 gm) cornflour
10$\frac{1}{2}$ oz (295 gm) can beef consommé or
  $\frac{3}{4}$ pint (425 ml) strong chicken stock
3 tablespoons water
1 oz (15 gm) sugar
1-1$\frac{1}{2}$ tablespoons Soy sauce
1 tablespoon vinegar

Set electric skillet to 300°F (150°C). Divide the cauliflower into flowerets, and cook in boiling salted water until *just* tender. Cook the beans in boiling salted water in a separate pan. Cut the meat into thin strips. Blend the sherry with a good pinch of salt and pepper in a basin. Add the meat, mix well with the seasoned sherry. Allow to stand for 10 minutes at room temperature.

Heat the oil in the pan, and brown the meat for 2-3 minutes. Blend together the cornflour and beef consommé or chicken stock; add to the meat with the water, sugar, Soy sauce, and vinegar. Cook, stirring until thickened. Add the cooked and drained cauliflower and beans. Stir until coated in the sauce. Heat thoroughly. Serve over boiled rice or noodles.
Serves 6.

TO VARY:
Other vegetables could be served with the beef instead of cauliflower and beans, try: baby carrots (leave whole, cook very lightly); sliced courgettes, or baby marrows.

Pork Sweet and Sour

Use lean pork instead of the sirloin steak. Cut this into thin strips, and proceed as the recipe above. One or two finely chopped dessert apples can be added to the sauce, or use well drained canned pineapple instead.

Steak Diane

Cooking time: 3-5 minutes

4 minute * steaks
salt and pepper
1 teaspoon dry mustard
2-3 oz (55-85 gm) butter
2 tablespoons lemon juice
2 teaspoons chopped chives
1 teaspoon Worcestershire sauce

*Use thin slices of rump or sirloin

Set electric skillet to 400°F (200°C). Sprinkle each side of the steaks with salt and pepper (freshly ground if possible), and a pinch of the dry mustard; press into the meat with a wooden spoon.

Melt the butter in the skillet. Add the steaks; cook 1-2 minutes on each side. Add the remaining ingredients to the pan; bring to boiling point, and spoon the sauce over the meat. Serve at once.
Serves 4.
NB: If a teaspoon of olive oil is added to the butter there is less chance of it becoming over-brown.

TO VARY:
1-2 tablespoons brandy can be added instead of, or with, the lemon juice.
2-4 oz (55-115 gm) mushrooms may be cooked with the steak in the recipe above, in which case increase the amount of butter slightly. The mushrooms look very attractive if fluted as in the picture (opposite).

TO FLUTE MUSHROOMS:

Cut away tiny strips of the peel of small culti-vated mushrooms as the sketch below.

Steak Diane is pictured opposite; this can be cooked in a very short time.

Sukiyaki

Cooking time: 10 minutes

1 lb ($\frac{1}{2}$ kilo) fillet steak, very thinly
   sliced across the grain
1$\frac{1}{2}$ tablespoons salad oil
1 oz (30 gm) sugar
6 tablespoons beef stock, canned
   condensed beef consommé, or water
   and $\frac{1}{2}$ beef bouillon cube
4 tablespoons Soy sauce
about 12 small bias cut spring onions,
   cut 2 in (5 cm) long
2-3 sticks celery, cut into slices 1 in
   (2 cm) long
2-4 oz (55-115 gm) thinly sliced
   mushrooms
5 oz (140 gm) canned water
   chestnuts, drained and thinly sliced
5 oz (140 gm) canned bamboo shoots,
   drained
4 oz (115 gm) torn fresh spinach
   leaves
16 oz (455 gm) can bean sprouts,
   drained
12-16 oz (340-455 gm) bean curd, cubed
   (optional, see below)

TO SERVE:
   hot cooked rice

Bean curd (tofu) may be found at Japanese food shops.

Set electric skillet to 375°F (190°C). Heat the meat in the oil for 1-2 minutes. Sprinkle with sugar. Blend the stock, consommé, or water and bouillon cube, and Soy sauce; pour over the meat. Push the meat to one side and allow the Soy mixture to bubble. Add the chopped onion and celery, keep these vegetables in separate heaps. Cook, tossing and stirring each of the three groups over the high heat for about 1 minute; then push to one side. Again keeping in separate groups, add the mushrooms, water chestnuts, bamboo shoots, spinach, bean sprouts, and bean curd. Cook and stir each food just until heated through. Serve with cooked rice, and Soy sauce if desired.
Serves 6.

BIAS CUT ONIONS

This means cut diagonally, giving a more attractive look to the finished dish.

Veal Bertrand

Cooking time: 15-18 minutes

4 oz (115 gm) fresh or canned
   mushrooms
salt
2 lb (1 kilo) veal fillet or cutlets
$\frac{1}{4}$ pint (140 ml) dry sherry
3 tablespoons chopped parsley
pinch of garlic powder
3 oz (85 gm) butter or margarine
3 slices processed Swiss cheese

Set electric skillet to 375°F (190°C). If using fresh mushrooms simmer for 4-5 minutes in salted water. Drain the vegetables. Canned mushrooms should also be drained. Cut the veal into 6-8 portions; pound to $\frac{1}{4}$ in ($\frac{1}{2}$ cm) thickness. Slash edges with a knife to prevent curling. Combine the mushrooms; sherry; parsley, and garlic powder. Pour mixture over meat. Marinate for 30 minutes, turning several times.

   Melt the butter or margarine in a pan or skillet. Drain the meat, reserving the mushroom marinade. Quickly brown half of the meat in the melted fat, for about 3 minutes on each side. Remove to warmed serving dish. Cook remaining meat for the same time. Return all meat to the pan. Reduce heat or re-set electric skillet to 275°F (140°C). Add the marinade and bring to boiling point. Reduce heat. Place cheese on top of meat. Cover; cook slowly for about 2 minutes only, until cheese melts. *Do not over-cook.* Transfer meat to warmed serving dish. Spoon hot sauce over.
Serves 6-8.
NB: If you want more sauce use $\frac{1}{4}$ pint (140 ml) sherry and $\frac{1}{4}$ pint (140 ml) chicken stock.

Weiner Schnitzel

Cooking time: 12-15 minutes

Coat thin fillets of veal with seasoned flour, beaten egg and crumbs, then fry in hot butter (or butter and oil) until crisp and golden. Top with slices of lemon and finely chopped hard-boiled egg and parsley.

Oriental Chi Chow

Cooking time: 15-20 minutes

- 1 lb ($\frac{1}{2}$ kilo) sirloin steak, 1 in (2 cm) thick
- 1$\frac{1}{2}$ tablespoons salad oil
- 8 oz (225 gm) mushrooms
- 5 oz (140 gm) canned bamboo shoots
- 5 oz (140 gm) canned water chestnuts
- 1 medium-sized onion
- 4-6 spring onions
- $\frac{1}{4}$ pint (140 ml) beef stock, or water and $\frac{1}{2}$ beef bouillon cube
- $\frac{1}{2}$-1 tablespoon sugar
- 2 teaspoons cornflour
- 1-3 tablespoons Soy sauce (see method)
- 1 tablespoon cold water
- 16 oz (455 gm) can sliced peaches, drained

TO SERVE:
Ginger Rice (see below)

Set electric skillet to 225-250°F (110-130°C). Slice the meat into thin strips. Heat the oil in the skillet then brown the meat. Add the sliced mushrooms, drained bamboo shoots, drained and sliced water chestnuts, chopped onion, beef stock, or water and bouillon cube, and sugar. Cover the pan and bring to simmering point, then cook for 5 minutes.

Blend the cornflour, some of the Soy sauce, and water. (Add the Soy sauce gradually as it has a very definite flavour.) Stir into the meat mixture. Cook, stirring constantly, until thickened; taste, add more Soy sauce as required, and the sliced peaches. Cover again and heat through; do *not* over-cook. Serve over hot Ginger Rice.
Serves 4-5.

Ginger Rice:
Mix 14 oz (400 gm) hot cooked rice with $\frac{1}{2}$ teaspoon ground ginger.

Because the infra-red rays from the top and bottom plates of the Infra-Red grill pictured opposite produce an intense radiant heat, grilling or cooking by this method is very quick.

Veal Cordon Bleu

Ham and cheese are sandwiched between the veal

Cooking time: 12 minutes

- 1-1$\frac{1}{4}$ lb (generous $\frac{1}{2}$ kilo) veal fillet, about $\frac{1}{4}$ in ($\frac{1}{2}$ cm) thick
- 4 thin slices ham
- 4 slices Gruyère cheese

COATING:
- 1 oz (30 gm) flour
- 1 egg, lightly beaten
- 2-3 oz (55-85 gm) fine dried breadcrumbs

FRYING:
- 2 oz (55 gm) butter or margarine
- 4 tablespoons dry white wine

Set electric skillet to 250°F (130°C). Do not exceed this as the veal 'sandwiches' are very thick. Pound each piece of veal until very thin (about $\frac{1}{8}$ in ($\frac{1}{4}$ cm) thickness). If necessary, trim slices of ham and cheese so that they are half the size of the veal pieces then halve each slice of veal. Top a veal piece with a slice of ham and cheese. Place another veal piece on top. Press edges together to seal. Repeat with remaining veal, ham and cheese.

Coat the meat with the flour. Dip in egg, then in breadcrumbs. In large skillet melt the butter or margarine. Brown the meat in the butter or margarine, over a medium heat, on both sides until golden brown (about 5 minutes on each side). Add the wine to the pan, stir well to absorb meat juice. Lift meat onto hot individual plates, then spoon wine over meat.
Serves 4.

Stuffed Ham Rolls

Served with a tangy pineapple sauce

Cooking time: 20-25 minutes

20 oz (570 gm) can pineapple spears
(see below)
3 tablespoons chopped onion
½ oz (15 gm) butter or margarine
½ packet (thyme and parsley or sage
and onion) stuffing mix
1 chicken bouillon cube
6 tablespoons boiling water
8 slices boiled ham
1 oz (30 gm) butter or margarine
2 oz (55 gm) sugar
1 tablespoon cornflour
pinch of salt
1 egg yolk, beaten

If pineapple spears are unobtainable buy pineapple cubes and use two or three in place of
spears.

Set electric skillet to 250°F (130°C). Drain
the pineapple, reserve scant ½ pint (¼ litre)
syrup; set aside. In a small frying pan, cook
the onion in the ½ oz (15 gm) butter or
margarine until tender; add the stuffing mix,
and the bouillon cube dissolved in the boiling
water.

Place 1 pineapple spear or several cubes on
a ham slice; spread with 2 tablespoons of the
stuffing mixture. Roll up; secure with a
wooden cocktail stick. Repeat with remaining
ham slices. Melt the 1 oz (30 gm) butter or
margarine in the electric skillet or large frying
pan. Add the ham rolls; cook for 10 minutes or
until heated through. Remove to a hot serving
dish.

Increase the skillet temperature to 375°F
(190°C). Combine the sugar, cornflour, and
salt, then add the reserved pineapple syrup. Stir
into the butter or margarine in the skillet, and
cook, stirring, until the sauce has thickened.
Gradually stir a small amount of the hot mixture
into the beaten egg yolk. Return to the skillet,
and cook for 1 minute more, stirring all the
time. Serve over ham rolls.
Serves 4.

TO VARY:
Omit the stuffing made with the onion, etc
and spread with French mustard instead. Use
cooked asparagus tips instead of pineapple
spears or cubes.

Ham in Sour Cream

Cooking time: 12-15 minutes

Set electric skillet to just below 250°F (120°C).
Melt 2 oz (55 gm) butter or margarine in the
skillet. Add 8-10 oz (225-285 gm) cooked
ham cut into juliènne strips (shreds about 1½
in (3 cm) long) and 6 tablespoons finely
chopped onion; cook until the onion is tender
but *not* brown. Add 3 oz (85 gm) chopped
mushrooms, and 1-2 tablespoons chopped
canned red pepper. Mix ¾ pint (425 ml) dairy
soured cream, and 4 tablespoons milk with 1
tablespoon flour; gradually stir into the ham
mixture. Simmer for 2-3 minutes or until the
mixture thickens (*do not boil*). Serve over hot
cooked rice, boiled noodles or cooked asparagus spears.

Serves 6-8.

Ham Rolls Soubise

Cooking time: 25 minutes

3 oz (85 gm) long grain rice
1 pint (570 ml) chicken stock
2 oz (55 gm) mushrooms, chopped
2 oz (55 gm) fresh or frozen peas
seasoning
12 tiny onions
1 oz (30 gm) flour
¼ pint (140 ml) thin cream
1 oz (30 gm) butter
2 oz (55 gm) Cheddar cheese, grated
(optional)
8 slices ham

Cook the rice in half of the stock with mushrooms, peas, and seasoning until it is of a sticky
consistency. Simmer the onions in the rest of
the seasoned stock until tender. Blend the
flour with the cream, stir into the onion mixture,
cook until thickened. Add the butter and
cheese, and heat gently. Spread the ham with
the rice mixture. Roll, and secure with wooden
cocktail sticks. Transfer the sauce to a shallow
pan over the table heater, add the ham rolls and
heat *without boiling*.

Serves 4.

Dinner by candlelight – Ham Rolls Soubise.

Cauliflower-Ham Salad

Cooking time: 10 minutes

1 small cauliflower
salt
2 tablespoons salad oil
$\frac{1}{2}$ oz (15 gm) sugar
2 teaspoons finely chopped or dried
  onion
1 teaspoon prepared mustard
$\frac{1}{2}$ teaspoon garlic salt
shake of pepper
$\frac{1}{4}$ pint (140 ml) water
4 tablespoons vinegar
1 teaspoon cornflour
6-8 oz (170-225 gm) cooked ham
1 small lettuce
4-6 tomatoes
2-3 sticks celery

Set electric skillet to 300°F (150°C). Separate cauliflower into small flowerets and boil in salted water until just tender (about 5-6 minutes). Meanwhile heat the oil and sugar, add the onion, mustard, garlic salt, $\frac{1}{4}$ teaspoon salt, and pepper. Blend the water and vinegar with the cornflour, pour into the skillet. Cook, stirring constantly, until the mixture thickens.

Add the cooked cauliflower and diced ham; heat through. Toss the shredded lettuce, sliced tomatoes, and chopped celery into the cauliflower mixture. Cook for 30 *seconds* longer. Serve immediately.
Serves 8.

Poultry Dishes

Many chicken and turkey dishes are ideal for tabletop cookery. Duck and goose, on the other hand, are less adaptable and generally better cooked in the kitchen, although the recipe opposite is very practical.

Young chickens may be barbecued (see page 77), or jointed, coated in seasoned flour, then egg and crumbs, and fried in either shallow fat or deep fat in the cooker shown left.

Chicken Aloha

Cooking time: 15 minutes

3-4 sticks celery
1 green pepper
1$\frac{1}{2}$ tablespoons salad oil
10$\frac{1}{2}$ oz (295 gm) can condensed cream
  of chicken soup
3 tablespoons water
1$\frac{1}{2}$ tablespoons Soy sauce
8 oz (225 gm) canned pineapple rings
1$\frac{1}{4}$-1$\frac{1}{2}$ lb (generous $\frac{1}{2}$-$\frac{3}{4}$ kilo) cooked
  chicken or turkey

TO SERVE:
cooked rice

GARNISH:
1 oz (30 gm) toasted slivered almonds

Set electric skillet to 250°F (130°C). Chop the celery, and cut the pepper into neat strips; discard the core and seeds. Heat the oil in a flame-proof pan or skillet, and cook the vegetables until just soft. Stir in the soup, water, and Soy sauce. Drain the pineapple, quarter each ring, add 6 tablespoons pineapple syrup, the pineapple pieces, and the neatly diced poultry. Cook, stirring occasionally, until hot. Serve over hot cooked rice. Garnish with the almonds.
Serves 6.

The deep cooker (left) is ideal for deep frying or making large quantities of stew or soups.

Turkey Hash

Makes good use of left over turkey

Cooking time: 20 minutes

2 oz (55 gm) butter or margarine
3 medium raw potatoes
3 tablespoons chopped onion
3 tablespoons chopped green pepper
½ pint (¼ litre) strong chicken stock,
 or water and 1 chicken bouillon
 cube
½ oz (15 gm) flour
½ pint (¼ litre) water
¼ teaspoon salt
pinch of dried rosemary leaves,
 crushed
shake of pepper
12 oz (340 gm) cooked turkey

GARNISH:
green pepper rings

Set electric skillet to 225°F (110°C). Melt the butter or margarine in the skillet. Peel and dice the potatoes. Toss the potatoes, onion, and chopped pepper in the butter or margarine for several minutes. Add the chicken stock, or water and bouillon cube and simmer for 5 minutes. Blend the flour and water, pour into the skillet, then add the salt, rosemary, and pepper. Continue cooking, stirring well, for another 5 minutes, then add the diced turkey. Cook until it is a thick mixture. If it becomes *too* thick, add extra stock or water. Top with rings of green pepper.
Serves 4.

Duck in Orange Sauce

Cooking time: 35 minutes

The cooking time is short because a cooked duck is used. Remove the peel from 2 oranges, discard the white pith, cut orange rind into thin strips, soak in 1 pint (½ litre) duck stock (made from the giblets). Tip into a pan, simmer for 20 minutes. Blend 1 oz (30 gm) cornflour with the orange juice, add to the stock with seasoning and 2 tablespoons red currant jelly, and simmer until smooth. Add the diced meat from 1 duck (discard most of the skin); keep hot over a table heater.
Serves 4.

Herbed Chicken Salad

Cooking time: a few minutes

2 small lettuces
1 lb (½ kilo) cooked chicken
1 oz (30 gm) Parmesan cheese, grated
DRESSING:
scant ½ pint (¼ litre) salad oil
5 tablespoons tarragon vinegar
1 teaspoon dry mustard
few drops Worcestershire sauce
shake of pepper
2 tablespoons chopped parsley

4 slices bread
2 oz (55 gm) butter or margarine

Tear the lettuces into bite-sized pieces and cut the chicken into neat cubes; mix with the lettuce and cheese. Blend together the dressing ingredients. Cut the bread into cubes, and fry in the hot butter or margarine until golden. Drain on absorbent paper. Toss the salad in the dressing and top with the croûtons.

Serves 6-8.

TO VARY:
Use other diced cooked poultry or game.

Chicken Scramble

Cooking time: 5-8 minutes

8 eggs, beaten
2 oz (55 gm) Cheddar cheese, grated
3 tablespoons milk
½ teaspoon salt
shake of pepper
4 oz (115 gm) cooked chicken
1½ oz (45 gm) butter or margarine
1 tablespoon chopped chives

Set electric skillet to 300-325°F (150-170°C). In a bowl combine the eggs, cheese, milk, and seasoning. Cut the chicken into thin strips. Melt the butter or margarine in the skillet. Add the chicken and chives, and cook, stirring for 2-3 minutes. Add the egg and cheese mixture. Cook, stirring occasionally, until the eggs are set.

Serves 6.

A JAPANESE DINNER

Tabletop cookery is not a novelty in Japan, for the food is cooked at the table there as part of the pattern of living.

Tempura is the main dish in this menu, but you could choose the equally famous Sukiyaki, page 64.

Arrange the ingredients attractively as shown in the picture opposite, but do not cook until almost ready to eat. The pan shown in the picture is not available in this country but the electric frying pans or flame-proof dishes would be equally as good.

The soup, which is cooked in a steamer, can be prepared beforehand and kept hot on a plate warmer, as can the rice. Do not over-cook rice if keeping warm as it continues to soften with standing.

MENU

Custard Soup

Tempura   Boiled Rice

Fresh Fruit

Saké or Sherry   Tea

Custard Soup

Cooking time: 35 minutes

6 spinach leaves
6 large prawns, peeled
2 oz (55 gm) mushrooms, sliced
6 water chestnuts, sliced
2 eggs
¾ pint (425 ml) chicken stock
seasoning

Shred the washed spinach finely, cover with boiling water, leave for 5 minutes, then strain. Put the prawns, spinach, mushrooms, and water chestnuts into six individual oven-proof soup cups or dishes. Beat the eggs, add the warmed chicken stock and seasoning.

Strain over the prawns, etc; cover the dishes with foil, and heat the soup for 30 minutes over hot water in a steamer until just set.
Serves 6.

Japanese Tempura

Cooking time: 2-3 minutes

18 raw large prawns, peeled
about 2 lb (1 kilo) assorted fresh vegetables such as asparagus, sweet potato, spinach, mushrooms, green beans
small bunch parsley

FRYING:
salad oil

BATTER:
4 oz (115 gm) flour
½ pint (285 ml) iced water
1 egg
1½ tablespoons salad oil
¼ teaspoon sugar
½ teaspoon salt

TO SERVE:
Tempura condiments (see method)

Set electric skillet or deep fryer to just below 375°F (180°C). Wash and dry the prawns and vegetables well. Cut the vegetables into strips, halve or quarter the prawns, divide the parsley into sprigs. Fill the skillet or deep fryer half full with oil. To make the batter, beat together flour, water, egg, oil, sugar, and salt. Meanwhile heat the oil.

Dip the prawns, parsley sprigs, and vegetables into the batter. Fry *steadily* in the hot oil until light brown; drain on absorbent paper.

Serve with Tempura condiments:
1 Grated fresh ginger root.
2 Grated whole peeled turnip and several large radishes blended together.
3 6 tablespoons prepared mustard mixed with 2 tablespoons Soy sauce.
Serves 6.

TO SERVE TEMPURA:
Dip the fried food into all the condiments. It is best if each person 'takes turns' in putting their coated food into the hot oil, then removes it and 'dips', while the second person fries some of the food. In this way there is no risk of any food being over-cooked or anyone burning themselves on the very hot cooking utensil.

Japanese Tempura with condiments.

Quick Snacks

SNACKS TO CHOOSE

When you are in a hurry one of the easiest and speediest of snacks is to serve savoury ingredients on toast.

Today there are attractive and relatively inexpensive toasters of various kinds that can be used in the dining-room for tabletop cookery, see below and page 76.

Egg, cheese, bacon, canned sardines, etc are some of the foods that blend with hot toast, but the recipes that follow also give more ambitious and original ideas. Remember toast is not improved with standing so have the other ingredients ready prepared to put onto the toast as quickly as possible.

Do not over-cook fillings and toppings containing cheese, for the cheese becomes tough and is easily spoiled. When using cheese for toasting choose Cheddar, Cheshire, Gruyère, Emmenthal, or Dutch cheeses. Processed cheese and Double Gloucester also heat well, in fact according to many records Double Gloucester was first used in Welsh Rarebit.

Where it is possible to pre-heat the grill or toaster beforehand do this, for it crisps the bread more quickly and cooks the topping better.

Crunchy Ham Sandwiches

Cooking time: 5-6 minutes

8 large slices white bread
little butter or margarine
little made mustard
4 slices boiled ham or boiled bacon
4 slices processed, Cheddar, or other cooking cheese
2-3 tomatoes

TO COAT:
2 eggs
2 tablespoons milk
pinch onion or garlic salt
about 4 tablespoons crushed potato crisps

Cover one side of the bread slices with butter or margarine and a little mustard. Top half of the slices with the ham or bacon, cheese, and sliced tomatoes, then another slice of buttered and mustard-spread bread.

Beat the eggs with the milk and salt, and put into a shallow dish. Cut the sandwiches into fingers or triangles, then dip into the egg mixture. Do this quickly, so the bread does not become too soggy. Put the crisps onto a plate or greaseproof paper and press the sandwiches into these. Toast until very crisp on either side. Serves 4.

Russell Hobbs Oven toaster

Crunchy Ham Sandwiches. Serve with salad.

German Sandwiches

Cooking time: 8-10 minutes

    2 oz (55 gm) butter or margarine
    1 tablespoon horseradish cream
    ½-1 teaspoon made mustard
    2 tablespoons finely chopped onion
    8 slices bread, preferably rye bread
    4 slices cooked ham or salami
    4 slices processed cheese

Blend the butter or margarine with the horse-radish cream, mustard, and onion. Spread both sides of the 8 slices of bread with the mixture. Top 4 slices with the ham or salami and cheese, then the other slices of coated bread. Put under a *warmed* grill or toaster. Do not have the heat too high for this particular sandwich. Cook on both sides until crisp, and the cheese begins to melt.

Serves 4.

TO VARY:
Add 1-2 teaspoons poppy seeds to the creamed butter mixture.
    Put the sandwiches into a pre-heated frying pan and fry instead of grilling.

Grilled Beefwiches

Cooking time: 8-10 minutes

    1 tablespoon very finely chopped
      spring onions or dried onion soup
      mix
    1 tablespoon horseradish cream
    pinch of pepper
    pinch of salt (do not use this with the
      soup mix)
    2 oz (55 gm) butter or margàrine
    8 large slices white bread
    4 large or 8 smaller slices cooked beef
    4 slices processed or Cheddar cheese

Blend the onions, horseradish cream, pepper, and salt with the butter or margarine. If using soup mix soften this first in 1 tablespoon water, then gradually blend with the ingredients. Spread both sides of the bread with the mixture. Top 4 slices with the beef, cheese, and the other slices of coated bread. Put under a *warmed* grill or toaster. Do not have it too hot for this sandwich. Cook on both sides until crisp and the cheese begins to melt.
Serves 4.
TO VARY:
Use cooked pork instead of beef and add a little chopped sage to the butter or margarine.

Welsh Rarebit

Cooking time: 5 minutes

2-2½ oz (55-70 gm) butter
pinch of salt
shake of pepper
shake of cayenne pepper
½-1 teaspoon made mustard
6-8 oz (170-225 gm) Cheddar or other
   cheese, grated (see page 72)
1 tablespoon Worcestershire sauce
1-2 tablespoons milk or ale
4-6 large slices bread

Cream 1½ oz (45 gm) of the butter and seasonings; add the cheese, then add the sauce gradually, to taste—many people like only a few drops. Stir in the milk or ale; if you like a very soft topping use the larger quantity. Toast the bread, spread with the remaining butter and add the cheese topping. Brown under the grill.
Serves 4-6.

Welsh Rarebit Relish

Cooking time: 10-12 minutes

2 oz (55 gm) mushrooms
1 small green pepper
2 oz (55 gm) butter or margarine
3 tablespoons finely chopped celery
1 oz (30 gm) flour
2 teaspoons prepared mustard
1 teaspoon Worcestershire sauce
about ½ pint (¼ litre) beer
1 lb (½ kilo) processed cheese,
   grated
Toast Cups (see page 54)

Chop the mushrooms and green pepper; discard the core and seeds. Melt the butter or margarine in a pan. Add the vegetables, and cook until tender; remove from the heat. Blend in the flour, mustard and Worcestershire sauce. Add the beer gradually. Bring to the boil and stir until thickened. Gradually add the cheese and cook, stirring until the cheese melts. If necessary, thin with a little extra beer. Keep mixture warm. Serve in Toast Cups.
Serves 4.

NB: A fondue pan is ideal for this.

Welsh Rarebit Variations

Welsh Rarebit is an excellent base for various additions. Those added in the picture on the following page are as follows:
Top left: Put rolls of boiled bacon or cooked ham on the rarebit, heat for 1-2 minutes if wished.
Top right: A traditional Welsh rarebit.
Middle left: Top with pickled onions.
Middle right: Grill rashers of bacon, make the Welsh rarebit and top with the bacon, heat for 1 minute if necessary.
Bottom left: Top the grilled cheese rarebit mixture with well drained sardines, return to the heat for 1-2 minutes.
Bottom right: Top the cooked Welsh rarebit with slices of raw tomato and heat for 1 minute only or top with a thick coating of sliced tomatoes and heat for several minutes until the tomatoes are soft.

Toasted Cheese

Instead of making a mixture as the rarebit left or below, top buttered toast with sliced Cheddar or other good cooking cheese, and heat for a few minutes until the cheese melts.

Cooked Rarebit Mixture

It is possible to make a cooked version of Welsh rarebit.

Cooking time: 10 minutes

Make a thick sauce with 1 oz (30 gm) butter, 1 oz (30 gm) flour and 6 tablespoons milk, or use 4 tablespoons milk and 2 tablespoons ale. Add salt, pepper, a little made mustard, and Worcestershire sauce to taste. Stir in 6 oz (170 gm) grated Cheddar or other cooking cheese; do not heat more than 1 minute to melt the cheese. Pour or spread onto buttered toast, and heat under the grill.
Serves 4-6.

The toppings opposite are described under Welsh Rarebit Variations above.

Chuck Wagon Macaroni

Cooking time: about 15 minutes
(depends upon macaroni)

6-7 oz (170-200 gm) macaroni
salt
2-3 oz (55-85 gm) butter or margarine
1-2 tablespoons chilli sauce
  (see below)
1 teaspoon Worcestershire sauce
8 oz (225 gm) strong Cheddar cheese,
  grated
paprika (optional)

Chilli sauce is *very* hot so add very gradually. Many people will like a few drops only.

In a large saucepan or flame-proof pan, cook the macaroni in salted water according to package directions; drain well. Return the cooked macaroni to the saucepan or flame-proof pan and place over the tabletop burner or cooker. Add the butter or margarine, chilli sauce, and Worcestershire sauce; heat, stirring until butter or margarine is melted. Add the cheese; stir until melted and well mixed. Sprinkle with paprika, if desired. Serve immediately.
Serves 4-6.

The picture below shows another practical electrical griller toaster. Reflected heat means that both sides of the food cook and brown simultaneously.

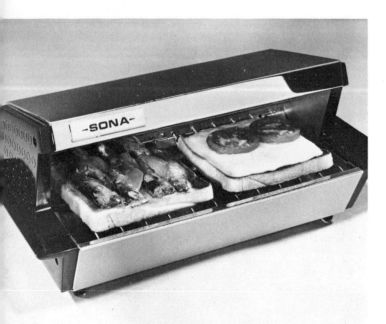

French Mushroom Omelette

An elegant egg dish

Cooking time: 5-6 minutes

3 eggs
1 tablespoon water
$\frac{1}{4}$ teaspoon salt
shake of pepper
pinch of mixed herbs
2-3 oz (55-85 gm) mushrooms, sliced
2 oz (55 gm) butter or margarine

Beat the eggs, water, salt, pepper, and mixed herbs until the mixture is blended but *not frothy*. Fry the mushrooms in half of the butter or margarine and keep warm in oven.

In an 8 in (20 cm) omelette pan heat the rest of the butter or margarine until it sizzles over the tabletop burner. Tilt the pan to grease sides. Pour in egg mixture, leaving heat moderately high. Allow to set for 30 seconds, tilt the pan, then swish the liquid egg to the sides. Cook until just set, about 2 minutes. Remove the pan from the heat; spoon the hot mushrooms over half of the omelette. With a wide spatula or palette knife lift and fold the omelette over the mushrooms. Slip out of the skillet onto a warm platter.

Serves 1-2.

NB: Other fillings may be used in the same way; make sure cooked fillings are very hot.

Hash-browns

Cooking time: 20 minutes

Set electric skillet to 250°F (130°C). Boil 6 medium-sized potatoes in their jackets; chill. Remove the peel and cut potatoes into thin strips. Mix with 2 tablespoons finely chopped onion; $\frac{1}{2}$ teaspoon salt, and a shake of pepper. Melt $2\frac{1}{2}$ oz (70 gm) butter or margarine in the skillet. Pack potatoes into the pan, leaving $\frac{1}{2}$ in (1 cm) space around edge. Cook for 10-12 minutes until golden coloured. Reduce heat if necessary. Cut into six wedges; turn over carefully. Cook for another 8-10 minutes on the second side.

Serves 6.

Indoor Barbecues

As you will have seen from the preceding pages, there are many fondues and other dishes suitable for tabletop cookery, so informal barbecues can be held indoors if the weather is not sufficiently good outside.

Traditional barbecue food should have a highly spiced flavour (or the main dish should provide this), so the barbecue sauce, opposite, can be used for basting food or to serve with it.

This particular menu is so simple children could prepare it for themselves.

MENU

Noodle-Bacon Scramble
Barbecued Chicken
Green Salad
Fresh Fruit
Beer, Cider, Coffee

Noodle-Bacon Scramble

Cooking time: 15 minutes

2 oz (55 gm) noodles
3 rashers bacon
4 eggs
2 tablespoons milk
½ teaspoon salt
shake of pepper
1 oz (30 gm) butter or margarine

Cook the noodles according to the package directions; drain. Cook the bacon until crisp, then crumble. Beat the eggs, milk, salt, and pepper until blended. Stir in the noodles and bacon.

Melt the butter or margarine in a pan. Add the egg-noodle mixture. Gently stir and fold, working from centre to outside. Continue cooking and folding until the eggs are cooked but still moist. Remove from the heat; serve immediately.
Serves 3-4.
NB: Cook the noodles and bacon beforehand.

Barbecued Chicken

Cooking time: from 15 minutes for jointed chicken to about 45 minutes or 1 hour

If you have a rotisserie, similar to the one illustrated on page 53, then leave the chicken whole. If you intend to cook the chicken over an habachi grill (page 53) or under the type of griller toaster on page 72 or the one opposite, then cut the chicken into joints. A small tender chicken should be divided into four, two breasts and wing pieces and two legs.

Barbecue Sauce

Cooking time: 6 minutes or no cooking

1 large onion, grated
3 tablespoons olive oil
2 tablespoons vinegar
2 level teaspoons cornflour
1-2 teaspoons Tabasco sauce (very hot)
2 tablespoons tomato ketchup or concentrated tomato purée
seasoning
2 teaspoons brown sugar

Toss the onion in the hot oil, then blend the vinegar and cornflour; add to the oil with the other ingredients and stir over a very low heat until the mixture thickens slightly. This can be kept warm and served with the cooked food. If you wish to use the sauce for basting omit the cornflour, blend all the ingredients together, and brush the chicken or other food with this as it cooks.

Serves 4-6.

TO VARY:

a Add 1-2 crushed cloves of garlic to the onion.

b Blend in 1-2 tablespoons chopped fresh herbs (parsley, chives, sage, etc).

c Add a little Worcestershire sauce as well as the Tabasco sauce.

Interesting Desserts

In addition to the fondue-type desserts on pages 38-42, here are other practical and interesting sweet dishes that may be heated or cooked at the table.

Some of the most spectacular are dishes where brandy or other liqueur or spirit are ignited. In order to make quite certain that the spirit will flame successfully, either pour into a separate pan and heat, then ignite and pour over the fruit, or pour the brandy into the cooking utensil, heat, then ignite. Naturally if you have too small a proportion of brandy to the other ingredients in the second method, it will not ignite. The dish tastes equally as good when not served flambé.

As heated sugar, etc reaches a very high temperature take special safety precautions.

Golden Sultana Flambé

Cooking time: 10 minutes

2½-3 oz (70-85 gm) sultanas
6 tablespoons brandy
1½ oz (40 gm) brown sugar
¼ teaspoon grated lemon peel
1 tablespoon lemon juice

TO SERVE:
vanilla ice-cream

Set electric skillet to 225°F (110°C). Put the sultanas and just enough water to cover into a pan. Bring the water to the boil, and simmer for 5 minutes. Drain the fruit and put into a basin. Add half of the brandy, the brown sugar, lemon peel, and lemon juice. Cover; leave to stand for 1 hour.

When serving, transfer sultana mixture to a skillet. Bring to boiling point. Heat the remaining brandy in a small pan. Ignite, then spoon over the sultanas. Serve the sauce over ice-cream.

Serves 6.

Cherries Jubilee

Cooking time: 10-12 minutes

2 15 oz (425 gm) cans cherries, preferably black
2-3 oz (55-85 gm) sugar
1 oz (30 gm) cornflour
5-6 tablespoons brandy or cherry brandy

TO SERVE:
vanilla ice-cream

Drain the cans of cherries, reserve the syrup. Blend the sugar, cornflour, and syrup in a basin, then pour into a pan and stir over a medium heat until mixture thickens. Stir in the cherries, then transfer the hot mixture to the container over the table heater. Keep warm until ready to serve.

If you wish to ignite the mixture, either warm the brandy in a small container then light it and pour over the cherry mixture, or pour the brandy into the cherry mixture, heat, then ignite. Serve the hot cherry mixture over vanilla ice-cream, see picture opposite.
Serves 10-12 (with ice-cream).

Hot Fruit Medley

Cooking time: 15 minutes

16 oz (455 gm) can pineapple chunks
15 oz (425 gm) can apricot halves
15 oz (425 gm) can peach halves
15 oz (425 gm) can black cherries
2 oz (55 gm) brown sugar
¼ teaspoon ground cinnamon
4 tablespoons port wine
1 tablespoon lemon juice

Drain the four cans of fruit. Put the syrup from the cans with the sugar, cinnamon, port wine, and lemon juice into the table cooker, and let this simmer until reduced to half the amount. Tip in the fruit and heat.

Serves 10-12.

Cherries Jubilee – luscious cherries in brandy sauce.

80

Cheese-filled Pears

Cooking time: 15 minutes

3 oz (85 gm) cream cheese
1 oz (30 gm) Danish Blue cheese
1 oz (30 gm) finely chopped nuts
scant ½ pint (¼ litre) water
2½ oz (70 gm) sugar
3 fresh pears, peeled, halved and
    cored (see below)
4½ tablespoons brandy
¼ teaspoon grated lemon rind
1 tablespoon lemon juice

Alternatively use canned pears with ½ pint (¼ litre) syrup from the can; omit water and sugar.

Blend the softened cream cheese and crumbled Blue cheese. Form into six balls, roll in nuts. Heat the water and sugar in a saucepan; poach the halved pears in this for 10 minutes. Pour the pear syrup, half of the brandy, the lemon rind, and the juice into a skillet or frying pan over a table heater. Fill each pear cavity with the cheese mixture, add to the liquid, heat gently. Warm the remaining brandy, ignite, pour over the pears and serve.
Serves 6.

Mandarin Pears

Cooking time: 10-12 minutes

8 large canned pear halves plus syrup
    from can
11 oz (310 gm) can mandarin oranges
1 level tablespoon cornflour
pinch ground cloves
pinch ground nutmeg
3 tablespoons orange marmalade
1 tablespoon lemon juice
½ oz (15 gm) butter
3 tablespoons orange juice or curacao

Drain the cans of fruit and reserve scant ½ pint (¼ litre) of the combined syrups. Blend the cornflour, ground cloves, ground nutmeg, and gradually stir in the reserved syrup. Add the marmalade, lemon juice and butter. Pour into a saucepan and cook steadily, stirring constantly, until thickened. Spoon into the serving dish over the table heater. Add the pear halves, cavity side uppermost. Place 3 or 4 mandarin orange segments in each pear cavity. Heat through, spooning sauce over the pears once or twice. Add the orange juice and heat, or the warmed curaçao, and ignite.
Serves 8.

Glorified Rice

Cooking time: 15 minutes

1 large can creamed rice (see below)
1 medium can crushed pineapple
    (see below)
2-3 tablespoons maraschino cherries
2 firm ripe bananas
1 lemon
3-4 oz (85-115 gm) marshmallows
½ pint (¼ litre) thick cream

The quantities of rice and pineapple can be adjusted according to personal taste.

Tip the rice and pineapple into a fondue pot or skillet over a table heater, stir to blend, warm gently. Add the cherries, the sliced bananas blended with lemon juice, and heat. Top with the marshmallows 5 minutes before serving, so these just melt. Serve with cream.
Serves 5-6.

Sauteéd Bananas

Cooking time: 5-8 minutes

4 large firm bananas
2 tablespoons lemon juice
2 eggs
2 tablespoons water
3 oz (85 gm) digestive biscuits
2 oz (55 gm) butter

Set electric skillet to 300°F (150°C). Cut each banana in quarters. Brush with lemon juice. Beat the eggs and water. Crush the biscuits to make fine crumbs. Dip bananas in the egg mixture, then in the biscuit crumbs. Put on a dish until ready to cook.
  Melt the butter in the skillet or frying pan. Add the pieces of banana, and fry until browned, turning once or twice. Serve hot with cream, ice-cream, or custard sauce.
Serves 4-6.

80

Rich Pancakes

4 oz (115 gm) flour, preferably plain
½ pint (¼ litre) milk
2 eggs
1 oz (30 gm) butter, melted
pinch of salt

FRYING:
little oil or butter

Set electric skillet to 250°F (130°C), for cooking Rich Pancakes. Blend all the batter ingredients. Beat until smooth. Grease skillet or 6 in (15 cm) omelette pan well, and heat. Spoon or pour in about 1½ tablespoons batter. Rotate the pan so the batter is spread evenly over the bottom; brown lightly on both sides, or for a softer pancake brown on one side only but make sure the batter is set. To remove, invert pan over kitchen paper. Repeat with remaining batter, greasing pan each time or adding a little oil or butter. Keep warm until serving.

Serves 6.

Apple and Nut Pancakes

Cooking time: 15 minutes

BATTER:
4 oz (115 gm) flour, preferably plain
½ pint (generous ¼ litre) milk
2 eggs
1 teaspoon grated lemon rind
2 teaspoons lemon juice
½ teaspoon vanilla essence

FRYING:
little oil or butter

FILLING AND SAUCE:
4 oz (115 gm) cream cheese
1½ oz (40 gm) pecans or walnuts, chopped
1 level tablespoon cornflour
¾ pint (425 ml) apple juice
2 teaspoons grated lemon rind
1 oz (30 gm) sugar (preferably brown)

DECORATION:
2 teaspoons coarsely grated or shredded lemon rind
1 oz (30 gm) chopped nuts

Set electric skillet to 225°F (110°C). Make the batter by blending all batter ingredients, then cook as Crêpes Suzette (page 83). Spread one side of the pancakes with the cream cheese (soften this with a little milk if too stiff), sprinkle with the nuts, then roll firmly. Blend the cornflour and apple juice, put into a pan with the lemon rind and sugar, and stir until thickened. Transfer to a skillet or shallow pan and heat, then add the pancakes and keep warm over a low heat. Top with the rind and nuts. Serves 6.

Hawaiian Pancakes

Cooking time: 15 minutes

ingredients as pancakes (see left)
15 oz (425 gm) can pineapple tidbits
½ oz (15 gm) cornflour
4 tablespoons orange juice
4 tablespoons honey
1 oz (30 gm) butter or margarine

Make and cook Rich Pancakes (page 81), pile onto a hot dish. Keep hot. Drain the pineapple, reserve the syrup; add enough water to the syrup to make a scant ½ pint (¼ litre). Blend the liquid with the cornflour, pour into a pan, bring to the boil, and stir until thickened. Add the pineapple, orange juice, honey, and butter or margarine. Bring to the boil, stirring constantly. Keep warm on a table heater. Spoon the sauce over the pancakes.
Serves 4-6.

TO VARY:
Use 1 tablespoon honey only, then the pancakes can be served with sausages or pork.

STORING PANCAKES

If you wish to make pancakes before they are required, store in the refrigerator or home freezer. A teaspoon of olive oil in the batter ensures that the pancakes do not become tough if kept for some time. Separate each pancake with waxed or greaseproof paper and wrap them all in a foil parcel. They keep for several days in a refrigerator or some weeks in a freezer.

Pancakes à la Mode

Cooking time: 15 minutes

ingredients for batter as recipe page 81
½ teaspoon ground cinnamon
½ teaspoon ground ginger
½ teaspoon ground nutmeg
1 tablespoon golden syrup

TO COOK:
butter or oil

TO SERVE:
vanilla ice-cream
Maple Syrup, see page 84
2 oz (55 gm) chopped pecans or other nuts

Prepare the pancakes as page 81, but sieve the spices with the flour; add the syrup, then the eggs and liquid. Cook the pancakes as page 81. Overlap two pancakes on each plate; top with a scoop of ice-cream, then Maple Syrup and nuts.
Serves 6-8.

Crêpes Suzette

RICH BATTER:
See page 81

FILLING AND SAUCE:
4 oz (115 gm) butter or margarine
4 oz (115 gm) sugar
2 teaspoons grated orange rind
1 teaspoon grated lemon rind
2 tablespoons orange juice
1 tablespoon lemon juice
icing sugar
3 tablespoons curaçao

Cook the pancakes in electric skillet (recipe Rich Pancakes page 81). Keep warm until ready to serve.

Cream the butter or margarine and sugar; add the grated rinds and fruit juices. Spread about 1 tablespoon cream filling on each pancake. Roll or fold; sprinkle with icing sugar.

When serving arrange filled pancakes in a skillet; heat slowly. In a small saucepan heat the liqueur. Ignite; spoon over crêpes.
Serves 6-8.

TO VARY:
Melt 2 ounces (55 grams) butter and 2 ounces (55 grams) sugar in frying pan, stir until sugar

A sumptuous feast of Crêpes Suzette.

has dissolved and heat until golden brown. Blend in 4 tablespoons orange juice, 2 table-spoons curacao then add the pancakes and heat gently. Ignite more curacao as above.

SAVOURY PANCAKES

Although many of the pancakes in this book are for desserts, remember they blend equally well with savoury ingredients; for example you can serve pancakes with many of the sauces on pages 23-29 or use pancakes instead of bread for dipping into fondue.

Curried Pancakes

Make the curry sauce as page 28 (either recipe), and blend with cooked diced meat, cooked chicken, or shell fish, kept hot.

Make and cook the pancakes, then spread the first pancake with the curry mixture, and cover with the second pancake. Continue like this, piling the pancakes high on top of each other. Serve with side dishes of chutney, sliced banana (dipped in lemon juice), chopped green and red peppers, desiccated coconut, sliced pineapple, etc.

Cottage Enchiladas

Cooking time: 15 minutes

ingredients for pancakes as page 81
12 oz (340 gm) cottage or cream cheese
scant ½ pint (¼ litre) soured cream
½ teaspoon salt
shake of pepper
10½ oz (295 gm) can enchilada sauce
8 oz (225 gm) Cheddar cheese, grated

Prepare and cook the pancakes as page 81; make a little smaller than usual. Blend cottage or cream cheese, soured cream, and seasoning. Fill the pancakes with half the mixture, and roll. Heat the sauce in a skillet over a table heater, stir in the rest of the filling and the Cheddar cheese; continue heating until the cheese has melted. Add the filled pancakes, and warm through.
Serves 4-6.

HOT SAUCES

These can be made at the table in a small pan or fondue pot over a table heater. In addition to the sauces given on this page try those below. Most of these sauces are ideal over pancakes, waffles, ice-cream, or plain sponge cakes.

Chocolate sauce: Break 4 oz (115 gm) plain chocolate or chocolate couverture into small pieces and melt *very slowly*. For a creamy flavour add 1-2 tablespoons cream, or for a new flavour a little brandy or orange juice. If the sauce is being kept hot for any length of time add 2-3 tablespoons water.

Mocha sauce: Add a little strong coffee to the chocolate.

Fudge sauce: Use fudge instead of chocolate. All sauces above serve 3-4.

Custard Sauce

Cooking time: 12-15 minutes

Mix 2 egg yolks, 1 egg and 2-3 tablespoons sugar. Whisk in 1 pint (½ litre) warmed milk, and ½ teaspoon vanilla essence. Cook slowly in the top of a double saucepan over hot, but *not boiling* water or in a strong pan over a very low heat, stirring well. Serve hot or cold. If serving cold, cool rapidly.

Serves 4-6.

Maple Syrup

Cooking time: 5 minutes

11 oz (310 gm) golden syrup
4 oz (115 gm) brown sugar
6 tablespoons water
½ oz (15 gm) butter or margarine

Put the syrup, sugar, and water in a small saucepan; heat, stirring constantly, until the sugar has dissolved. Add the butter or margarine, and boil for 1 minute.

Makes generous ½ pint (¼ litre).

Caramel Sauce

Cooking time: 5-6 minutes

Put 6 oz (170 gm) granulated, caster, or loaf sugar into a strong pan with 6 tablespoons water. Stir over a low heat until the sugar has melted, then boil *without stirring* until golden brown.

Serves 4-5.

Nutmeg-Pineapple Sauce

Cooking time: 10 minutes

4 oz (115 gm) white sugar
4 oz (115 gm) brown sugar
3 tablespoons golden syrup
2 oz (55 gm) butter or margarine
½ teaspoon ground nutmeg
¼ teaspoon vanilla essence
13½ oz (385 gm) can pineapple tidbits

Heat all the ingredients except pineapple until the sugars have melted, stir well to prevent mixture scorching. Boil steadily for a few minutes, then tip in the well drained pineapple, and heat. This is particularly good over waffles, pancakes, and fingers of plain sponge cake. It is a little sweet to serve over ice-cream.

Serves 6-8.

Peach Sauce

Cooking time: 12-15 minutes

1 lb 13 oz (¾ kilo) can peach slices
1 oz (30 gm) cornflour
1 oz (30 gm) butter or margarine
1 tablespoon lemon juice
2 tablespoons orange juice
1 teaspoon grated orange rind
1 teaspoon grated lemon rind
¼ teaspoon ground nutmeg

Drain can of peach slices. Blend the syrup with the cornflour, pour into a pan. Add all ingredients except peach slices. Cook steadily, stirring well until mixture thickens. Add the peaches, and heat.

Serves 8-10.

Making Waffles

Waffles, like pancakes, can be served as an accompaniment to both savoury and sweet ingredients. In addition, waffles are suitable for most meals, from breakfast (with bacon) to fruit or jam topped waffles as a dessert. Waffle irons, as the model shown on this page, are neat and attractive, and an ideal piece of equipment for tabletop cookery.

When using a new waffle iron read and follow the manufacturer's instructions carefully. You may find it necessary to brush the inside of the iron with melted fat or oil before using it for the first few times. After this you should be able to cook the waffles in the hot iron, without using much, if any, oil or fat.

Serve waffles as soon as they are cooked. The waffle batter may be prepared beforehand, then given a brisk stir before using. If the recipe contains stiffly whisked egg whites, as below, add these at the last minute.

Basic Waffles

Cooking time: 2-3 minutes for each waffle

- **7 oz (200 gm) plain flour**
- **3 level teaspoons baking powder**
- **pinch of salt**
- **2 egg yolks, beaten**
- **¾ pint (425 ml) milk**
- **4 tablespoons salad oil, melted fat, or butter**
- **2 egg whites, stiffly beaten**

Sieve together the flour, baking powder, and salt. Gradually beat in the egg yolks, milk, and salad oil, fat, or butter. Allow this to stand until ready to cook. Fold in the stiffly beaten egg whites.

Heat the waffle iron. Spoon in enough batter to give a thin coating. Cook until the waffles are crisp and golden. Remove the waffles from the iron. Serve with a sauce or accompaniments. Serves 4-6.

TO VARY:
Do not separate the egg whites and yolks.

A modern electric waffle iron.

TOPPINGS FOR WAFFLES

The following make excellent accompaniments to waffles. Prepare the ingredients and have them all ready before cooking the waffle mixture in the hot iron.

SAVOURY TOPPINGS

Cottage and pepper waffles: Blend cottage cheese with a little mayonnaise, a squeeze of lemon juice, seasoning, and chopped red or green pepper. Spoon on the hot waffles.

Ham and tomato waffles: Simmer chopped skinned tomatoes until they form a thick purée. Blend with chopped cooked ham and seasoning.

Sausage and apple waffles: Core, but do not peel cooking apples, then cut into slices. Fry sausages until golden brown and cooked, keep hot, then fry the apple rings in the fat in the pan. Put the apple rings on the hot waffles, and top with the sausages.

SWEET TOPPINGS

Simmer fruit, with a little sugar, until it is a smooth purée, or heat canned fruit, drain well then serve on the waffles.

Heat jam or marmalade, or spoon honey, golden syrup or black treacle over the waffles. The Maple Syrup recipe on page 84 is excellent if you cannot obtain it ready prepared. Ice-cream with fresh fruit is another simple, but excellent topping.

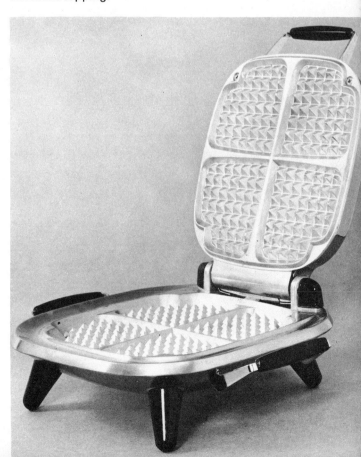

Chocolate Dot Waffles

Cooking time: 2-3 minutes for each waffle

waffle batter as page 85
6 oz (170 gm) package plain chocolate dots

TO SERVE:
¼ pint (140 ml) thick cream
1-2 oranges

Make batter as page 85. Pour some of the batter onto the preheated waffle iron. Sprinkle each unbaked waffle with the chocolate dots or neat pieces of broken chocolate. Cook the waffles. Top each serving with a little whipped cream and segments of orange or shredded orange rind, as illustrated.
Serves 4-6.

The picture shows the Chocolate Dot Waffles, recipe above.

Gingerettes

Cooking time: 2-3 minutes for each waffle

12 oz (340 gm) gingernut crumbs
2 teaspoons baking powder
½ teaspoon salt
scant ½ pint (¼ litre) milk
3 egg yolks, beaten
2 oz (55 gm) butter, melted
3 egg whites, stiffly beaten
vanilla ice-cream
sliced canned or fresh sweetened peaches

Blend crumbs, baking powder and salt. Beat the milk, egg yolks, and butter gradually into the crumbs. Only fold in the whites *just* before cooking. Cook in the pre-heated waffle iron. Top with ice-cream and peaches.

Serves 8.

NO-COOK MENU

Although this book has specialized in dishes to cook at the table, the following menu can be served at the table and it requires no cooking. It is ideal, therefore, for older children to make for their friends. The chocolate haystack ingredients are heated and allowed to set, so make these some time before being required.

MENU

Onion Dip
Tomato Shrimp Dip
Chef's Salad in a Roll
Chocolate Haystacks
Cider   Iced Coffee

Chef's Salad in a Roll

Quick and easy to assemble

No cooking

4 long rolls
butter or margarine
4 oz (115 gm) Cheddar or Gruyère
   cheese
1 round or Cos lettuce
4 slices ham
4 slices salami
2 hard-boiled eggs, sliced
French dressing

Split the rolls lengthwise, cutting *to* but not through crust at back. Spread cut surfaces of rolls with butter or margarine. Cut the cheese into match-stick shapes.

For each sandwich : Cover bottom half of roll with well washed and dried lettuce, then a few cheese strips and a slice of ham and salami, each folded in half. Place egg slices on top of meat. Moisten each sandwich with about ¼ tablespoon French dressing just before serving. Anchor tops of rolls with wooden cocktail sticks if necessary.
Serves 4.

Chocolate Haystacks

Cooking time: 5-6 minutes

1 lb (½ kilo) sugar
6 tablespoons milk
4 oz (115 gm) butter or margarine
2 oz (55 gm) unsweetened cocoa
   powder
12 oz (340 gm) quick cooking rolled
   oats
3 oz (85 gm) desiccated coconut
2 oz (55 gm) walnuts, chopped
½ teaspoon vanilla essence
pinch of salt

Blend the sugar, milk, butter or margarine and cocoa powder in a saucepan. Bring to the boil, stirring once or twice. Remove from the heat. Stir in the rolled oats, coconut, walnuts, vanilla essence and salt. Drop quickly from a teaspoon onto greaseproof paper; cool.
Makes about 48 haystacks.

The Onion Dip above is made by blending cottage cheese and salad cream with a little seasoning, lemon juice, and finely chopped spring onions (chives could be used). The Tomato Shrimp Dip is made in the same way, but chopped shrimps and a little tomato ketchup are added. If preferred, use potted shrimps in the dip.

A CONTINENTAL TOUCH

Two of the most famous continental dishes are ideal for cooking at the table. The Risotto (rice dish) from Italy and the Paella (that delicious mixture of rice and seafoods) from Spain should be eaten when *just* cooked so that you can be certain of these dishes at their very best.

Risotto alla Finanziera

Cooking time: 30 minutes

3 oz (85 gm) butter or margarine
2 small onions, chopped
4 medium-sized tomatoes, skinned and chopped
2-4 oz (55-115 gm) mushrooms, thinly sliced
8-10 oz (225-310 gm) Italian or long grained rice
about 6 chicken livers
3 pints (good 1½ litres) chicken stock
seasoning
grated Parmesan cheese

Heat the butter or margarine in a large pan, stir in the vegetables, and cook for several minutes. Add the rice and turn in the mixture, then add the diced chicken livers and the stock. Bring to the boil, stir briskly, then transfer to the table heater and allow to cook steadily, without covering the container, until the rice is nearly tender and the liquid absorbed. Taste, and season well. Serve topped with the grated cheese.
Serves 4-6.

TO VARY:
a Omit the livers and use tiny pieces of chicken, ham, or fish.
b Add diced pepper (red or green) and a few sultanas to the recipe. Put in the pepper with the onions; add the sultanas towards the end of the cooking period.

Paella de Marascos

Cooking time: 35 minutes

pinch of saffron or a few strands of saffron
1½ pints (nearly 1 litre) chicken stock
2 tablespoons olive oil
1 medium-sized onion, chopped
1-2 cloves garlic, crushed
6 oz (170 gm) long grained rice
1 small lobster
12 large shelled prawns (approximately)
seasoning

If using saffron powder, add it to the chicken stock; if using saffron strands, infuse them in the stock for about 30 minutes, and strain just before using. Heat the oil in a large pan (ideally one should cook and serve in the same pan), then toss the onion and garlic in the oil for a few minutes. Add the rice and mix with the onion mixture, then add the stock and cook steadily until the liquid comes to the boil. Stir briskly, then transfer to a table heater. Add the diced lobster meat and prawns, season, and heat until the rest of the liquid is absorbed and the fish is hot.

Serves 3-4.

TO VARY:
The above recipe is only one of the many versions of Paella which vary according to the region of Spain. The most famous, often just called Paella, or Arroz a la Valenciana, is made as the recipe above, but a young chicken, cut into small pieces, is fried with the onion, then diced Chorizo sausage, mussels, cooked peas, as well as shell fish are added to the rice. You must increase the amount of stock to 2 pints (nearly 1¼ litres) for the slightly longer cooking period. The exact proportions of sausage, etc are a matter of personal taste.

Beverages

To round-off a pleasant meal cooked or served at the table, have some kind of coffee maker that may be used in the dining-room, or if you prefer tea as a beverage have a small portable electric kettle so that tea may be made at the table. Chocolate or cocoa drinks may be prepared in a ceramic fondue pot.

When making coffee choose the right type of coffee for the particular coffee maker. Most percolators require a medium ground coffee; if it is too fine the water cannot percolate through the ground coffee; if it is too coarse you have a poor and weak brew.

MAKING GOOD COFFEE

Whatever kind of coffee maker you choose there are certain basic points to remember:

1. Always use freshly ground coffee. If you buy the vacuum sealed tins of coffee make certain the lid is replaced immediately after use, so the coffee does not lose its strength and fresh flavour.
2. Draw the water freshly; use water from the cold, and not the hot tap.
3. Allow the right amount of coffee—to give a pleasantly strong brew allow 4 level (2 heaped tablespoons) coffee to each 1 pint (generous $\frac{1}{2}$ litre) of water.
4. Many modern electric percolators or coffee makers are thermostatically controlled, so that the coffee does not boil rapidly after it has been made. The coffee should infuse *gently*. Over-boiling produces a bitter taste to the drink.
5. Serve cold or hot milk or cream with the coffee. *Never* boil the milk, for this gives a definite and less pleasant taste to the drink—it also gives an unattractive skin.
6. Ideally coffee should be served in warmed cups, although this is not often done; the warmers for Irish (Gaelic) coffee glasses shown opposite ensure a most pleasant drink.

This Paella is in a flame-proof dish that can be used on any type of cooker, also as a serving dish. The handle is removable.

The picture above shows a modern electric automatic percolator. The heat is controlled so the coffee does not over-boil.

Party Drinks

Irish Coffee

Warm the glasses, add the desired measure of Irish whiskey. Top with strong, hot coffee. Finally pour thick cream over the spoon, as shown in the picture, below. If Scotch whisky is used, the drink is known as Gaelic coffee.

Heaters for Irish coffee glasses. These heaters are also excellent for warming brandy glasses.

Café Brûlot

Cooking time: 8 minutes

12 sugar cubes
1 tablespoon shredded orange peel
1 teaspoon shredded lemon peel
4 in (10 cm) stick cinnamon
3-4 whole cloves
¼ pint (140 ml) cognac
1½ pints (¾ litre) strong hot coffee

Mix the sugar, orange and lemon peels, cinnamon and cloves. Add half the cognac, heat, then ignite. Combine the remaining cognac and coffee. Stir into the spice mixture. Ladle into small coffee cups.
Serves 8.

Party Punch

A hot punch is traditionally served in a large bowl. If this is of silver the drink may be kept hot on a plate warmer or over a table heater. When a proper punch bowl is not available, large ceramic bowls may be used instead, but take care they are sufficiently heat-proof to be kept hot for a long period. Ceramic fondue pots could be used for smaller quantities of a hot drink.

> **2 large oranges**
> **2 large lemons**
> **½ pint (¼ litre) water**
> **4 oz (115 gm) sugar**
> **3 pints (good 1½ litres) ginger ale**
> **1 pint (½ litre) brandy**
> **1-2 oz (30-55 gm) crystallized ginger**

Pare the rinds from the fruit. Put into the pan with the water and sugar, and simmer for 10 minutes. Strain off the rinds, then return the syrup to the pan with the ginger ale and fruit juices; bring to the boil. Add the brandy and the sliced crystallized ginger, and pour into the heated punch bowl.
Fills 12-14 punch cups.

Cider Snap

Cooking time: 5 minutes

> **2 pints (1 litre) apple cider or apple juice**
> **2 oz (55 gm) glacier mints**

DECORATION: (optional)
> **unpeeled apple slices**
> **cinnamon sticks**

Heat the cider or apple juice and mints in a pan until the sweets are dissolved and the cider or apple juice is hot. Pour into mugs. Top each serving with an unpeeled apple slice and piece of cinnamon stick, if desired.
Serves 6-8.

Questions and Answers

Q Why is it so important to keep the heat low under a fondue?
A If the oil is allowed to become too hot food could burn and the oil could be dangerous as if it becomes *very hot* it ignites. If the cheese mixture becomes too hot the mixture will curdle (ie separate).

Q What can be done if the oil gets over-heated?
A Remove pan of oil from the heat or turn off the heat; allow the oil to cool. When oil is badly or consistently over-heated it does develop an unpleasant taste.

Q Is there any remedy if the cheese mixture does curdle?
A Whisk very sharply, then whisk in 1 table-spoon lemon juice (this often helps to restore the original creamy texture). If the mixture is emulsified in a warmed liquidizer it may restore the smooth texture, but there is always a tendency for the cheese mixture to curdle again.

Q If a cheese fondue mixture becomes too stiff what should one do?
A *Gradually* add a little more wine.

Q Emmenthal and Gruyère cheeses are very similar in flavour; how can one tell the difference when buying these, if they are not labelled?
A Emmenthal is the cheese with the bigger holes. Although similar in texture and flavour, the use of *both* cheeses in a fondue gives an excellent result.

Q Is it possible to make a fondue or other 'table cooker' dishes without the special equipment?
A Yes, all recipes in this book can be prepared on an ordinary cooker, providing care is taken to keep the heat low. If cheese fondues are kept hot over very hot water they will keep a good consistency, but the cheese mixture does cool and become tougher if the hot water is not renewed very frequently.

Index

BASIC METHODS OF COOKING

BAKING—cooking in dry heat in the oven.

BOILING—cooking food in a boiling liquid (212°F), eg. vegetables, pasta and boiled puddings.

BRAISING—meat is browned then cooked slowly on a bed of vegetables with very little liquid, in a covered container.

FRYING—Shallow frying is cooking in just enough fat to cover the base of the pan. It is a quick method of cooking.
    Deep frying is cooking food by immersing in a deep pan filled two-thirds full of hot fat or oil.

GRILLING—always pre-heat the grill for this method of cooking and brush the grill rack with fat. Food which is to be completely cooked by grilling should be cooked at a high temperature for the initial browning period. Then reduce the heat and complete the cooking.

POACHING—cooking food gently in liquid at simmering temperature (185-200°F).

POT ROASTING—a combination of frying and steaming. The meat is browned and then cooked in a heavy covered casserole or saucepan with fat only. It is a slow method of roasting and may be carried out on top of the stove or in the oven at a low temperature.

PRESSURE COOKING—cooking food at a very high temperature under pressure. The food cooks quickly and tougher types of meat are made more tender. Types of pressure cookers vary and the makers instructions should be followed exactly.

ROASTING—cooking food at a high temperature in the oven. The container is open and little fat should be used.

SAUTÉ—To cook over a strong heat in a small amount of fat or oil, shaking the pan frequently to prevent sticking.

SIMMERING—cooking below boiling point—the liquid should bubble gently at the side of the pot.

STEAMING—using the steam from boiling water to cook food. The food may be cooked in a steamer over boiling water or the basin of food may be stood in the boiling water. Always cover the saucepan or steamer.

STEWING—cooking food at simmering point or below in a liquid. It is a long slow method of cooking and an excellent way of tenderising the tougher cuts of meat. Stewing is carried out in a covered container.

COOKING TERMS

BAIN MARIE—a roasting tin half filled with water in which a dish of food which must be baked slowly is placed before cooking in the oven, e.g. caramel custards.

BAKING BLIND—the method of baking flans, tarts and other pastry cases without a filling. Put the flan ring or pie dish on a baking sheet and line with pastry. Cut a circle of greaseproof paper slightly larger than the flan. Fill with dried beans, rice, or bread crusts to weigh the paper down. Bake the flan for 15 minutes. Remove the greaseproof paper and beans and bake a further 10 minutes to brown and crisp the pastry. Cool.

BASTING—spooning the cooking fat and liquid over food while roasting. This keeps the food moist, adds flavour and improves the appearance.

BEATING—method of introducing air to a mixture, a wooden spoon, wire whisk or electric beater may be used for this process.

BINDING—adding a liquid, egg or melted fat to a dry mixture to hold it together, e.g. beaten egg is added to mince for hamburgers.

BLANCHING—putting food in boiling water in order to either whiten, remove the skin, salt or strong flavour from food.

BLENDING—the process of mixing a thickening agent, such as flour or cornflour with a little cold water to a smooth paste. A little of the hot liquid to be thickened is then added to the paste and the whole returned to the saucepan. The mixture is stirred until it boils and thickens. Used to thicken the liquid of casseroles, stews and certain sauces.

BOUQUET GARNI—a bunch of fresh mixed herbs tied together with string and used for flavouring. Usually a bay leaf, sprig of parsley, sprig of thyme and perhaps a few celery leaves. Dried herbs may be used tied in a little muslin bag.

BROWNING—putting a cooked dish or meringue under the grill, or in the oven for a short time to give it an appetising golden colour.

CASSEROLE—baking dish usually ovenproof earthenware, pottery, porcelain or cast-iron with a tight fitting lid. Food cooked in a casserole is served straight from the dish.

CHINING—method of preparing neck or loin joints for easier carving. The bone at the wide end of the chops or cutlets is cut away from the meat so that it may be carved into portions of one rib each.

CHOPPING—dividing food into very small pieces on a chopping board using a very sharp knife.

COATING—covering food with a thin layer of flour, egg, breadcrumbs or batter before it is fried.

CONSISTENCY—term describing the texture (usually the thickness) of a mixture.

CREAMING—beating together fat and sugar to incorporate air, break down the sugar crystals and soften the fat.

CUTTING IN—Usually applies to adding fat to pastry. Fat is cut into flour with a knife.

FOLDING IN—to incorporate two mixtures using a light over and over motion. Usually applied to light mixtures such as whisked egg white or cream which have to be folded into other ingredients. It is important to carry out the process carefully so that the air is not knocked out of the light mixture. Flour is sifted over whisked egg mixtures for very light sponge cakes. The use of an electric mixer is not practical for this process. A sharp edged metal spoon is ideal for folding in.

GLAZE—a liquid brushed over the surface of a dish to give it a shiny finish.

GRATE—shaving food into shreds.

HULL—remove stalks from soft fruits—strawberries, raspberries etc.

KNEADING—working a dough using the fingertips for pastry-making and the knuckles for bread-making. The edges of the dough are drawn to the centre.

KNOCKING BACK—This applies to yeast mixtures which have had one rising. The dough is turned out, kneaded with the hands and reshaped.

MARINADE—a liquid made of oil and wine, vinegar or lemon juice and flavouring vegetables, herbs and spices. Food is steeped in the marinade to tenderise and add flavour.

PURÉE—fresh or cooked fruit or vegetables are broken down into a smooth pulp by sieving, pounding or blending in the liquidiser.

REDUCING—boiling a liquid, uncovered, in order to evaporate the water content and make the liquid more concentrated.

ROUX—a thickening agent for soups and sauces. Equal quantities of fat and flour are cooked together.

RUBBING IN—a method of incorporating fat into flour, e.g. in short-crust pastry making. Add the fat in small pieces to the flour. Using the fingertips, quickly and lightly rub the fat into the flour, lifting the hands as you do this.

SEASONED FLOUR—mix 1 teaspoon of salt, a good sprinkling of pepper and 2 tablespoons flour. Use to coat food before cooking.

SIEVING—to rub food through a sieve using a wooden spoon, in order to discard skin, stalks or seeds.

SKIMMING—to remove the scum or fat from food whilst it is cooking. A piece of absorbent kitchen paper or a metal spoon are used.

STOCK—a well-flavoured liquid made by simmering meat and/or vegetables in water for a prolonged period, to extract the flavour. When time is short the commercial stock cubes may be substituted.

SWEATING—cooking foods, usually vegetables in a small amount of fat to soften and add flavour. The pan is always covered.

WATER BATH—see Bain marie.

WHIPPING OR WHISKING—adding air quickly to a mixture by beating with a hand whisk, rotary beater or electric beater.

ZEST—the thin coloured skin of citrus fruit which contains the oil and flavour.